FOUR MILE RUN LAND GRANTS

Charles W. Stetson

HERITAGE BOOKS
2019

HERITAGE BOOKS

AN IMPRINT OF HERITAGE BOOKS, INC.

Books, CDs, and more—Worldwide

For our listing of thousands of titles see our website
at
www.HeritageBooks.com

A Facsimile Reprint
Published 2019 by
HERITAGE BOOKS, INC.
Publishing Division
5810 Ruatan Street
Berwyn Heights, Md. 20740

International Standard Book Numbers
Paperbound: 978-1-58549-365-4
Clothbound: 978-0-7884-6865-0

CONTENTS

THE HOWSING PATENT

On October 21st, 1669 Sir William Berkeley, Governor of Virginia, issued a patent to Robert Howsing for six thousand acres "being upon the freshes of Potomack River on the west side thereof above the dividing branches of ye same beginning at a red oake standing by a small branch or a run of water neare opposite to a small Island commonly called and known by the name of My Lords Island extending downe Potomack River various courses 3152 po. making a Southwesterly line to a pokecory standing at the north point of a creek named by the English Indian Cabin Creeke wch Creeke divides this land and a tract of land surveyed for Jno. Mathewes, from the said pokecory Northwest and by West up the said Creeke and maine Branch 520 po. from thence North 1940 po. finally East 720 po. to the red oake begun at, including sev'all small creekes or inlets for the said quantity. The said land being pr Trans of 120 psons etc. ... Yeilding and paying etc." [1] The names of the persons are appended to the patent. Howsing was the master of the ship that brought these emigrants, and was entitled under the existing headwright law to a grant of fifty acres for every settler he brought into the colony. [2]

Howsing assigned his patent to John Alexander by a deed dated October 13/1669 recorded in Stafford County. The consideration is said to have been six hogsheads of tobacco, but the record of the deed is lost. It is evident that the land had been selected by Alexander before the patent

---

[1] Land Patents 6-262.

[2] The head right legislation was designed to secure a steady flow of immigration into the colony. It also "furnished practical assurance that the appropriation of the soil would not outstrip too far the growth in the number of the inhabitants".

Economic History of Virginia, Bruce 1-514.

was issued.   He was a surveyor as well as a planter and had been recently in the freshes of the Potomac River surveying the future Mt. Vernon estate for Col. John Washington and Col. Nicholas Spencer.   Howsing had no occasion to sail up the river above the settlements.   He was a sailor and his concern was to turn his patent into merchandise as quickly as possible.   No survey is recited in the patent, and the subsequent difficulties in applying the description to the ground showed none was made.

The tract was a wilderness uninhabited by white men. The Doeg and Necostin Indians hunted over it and the site of a small Indian village has been located near the mouth of Four Mile Run.   The Indians were then at peace with the colonists, but it is unlikely Alexander considered it worth while to venture two miles inland on no more important business than surveying a tract that would not be occupied for some years.   The north boundary of the patent is the line bounding Arlington Cemetery and Fort Myer on the north.   My Lords Island has borne various names, Barbadoes, Mason's, Analostan and now Roosevelt.   The name Analostan first appears on Augustine Herman's Map of Maryland in 1670 as "Anacostian Isle".   The small branch at the beginning point of the patent is designated on an early survey as Wampakan Branch, but has no name today.   It drains the northerly half of Arlington Cemetery. The southerly boundary is Great Hunting Creek, called Indian Cabin Creeke in the patent, and Mussell Creek in other early patents.   Alexander's mistaken notion that the Potomac River flowed in a southwesterly direction between Analostan Island and Hunting Creek led to the error of assigning a greater length to the northern boundary than to the southern.   The "pokecory" trees designated as boundaries were hickory trees, natives of North America.   The Indian name is usually given as pohickory.   Pohick run and church derive their name from the tree.

John Alexander came to Virginia from Scotland shortly after the middle of the seventeenth century.   His first grant of land was in Northampton County on the Eastern

2

Shore. In 1664 he patented 1450 acres on the Potomac River, in what was then Westmoreland County, and is now King George, to which he gave the name of Salisbury. It was there he made his home and there his descendants lived until the Civil War. An ancient brick dwelling, one and a half stories, bearing the name of Caledon still stands on part of the tract. It is said to be part of a larger building erected about 1725 by a grandson. It is near the Potomac River about twenty miles east of Fredericksburg, in the region once called Chotank.

The Alexander family claims descent from Sir William Alexander, Earl of Stirling. [3] John Alexander had three sons, John who died in his father's lifetime without issue, Robert and Philip. On October 5th, 1677 he made an unsigned will bequeathing to Elizabeth Homes "200 acres where John Coggins lives", to John Dry 500 acres "being the northermost part of the 6750 acres on the freshes of the Potomac River", and all the rest of his estate to his sons Robert and Philip. The Stafford records where the attempted will was recorded are destroyed but a copy of the will is preserved as an exhibit in the suit of Alexander vs Birch. [4]

In 1690 Robert Alexander conveyed to his younger brother, Philip, a half interest in the land embraced in the Howsing patent. A copy of the deed filed, in Alexander vs Birch, recites that their father John Alexander by his will dated October 5th, 1677 devised all the remainder of his estate to his two sons, "which will though it fully manifests the testator's intention, yet John Alexander going about to sign it, was by his sudden death prevented". The attempted devise to John Dry was not confirmed, and he disappears from the Howsing patent, but the 200 acres given to Elizabeth Homes must have been confirmed to her, as the report of the Surveyor in Alexander vs Birch shows

---

[3] William and Mary College Quarterly 8–164.

[4] District Court of Dumfries, Land Suits 1 p 89. The volume is now in the office of the clerk of Prince William County.

3

he was directed to locate it, as a part of the patent. It is the 200 acres on Hunting Creek shown on the survey of 1741 (See page 10) as "Mr. Harrison's land". She was probably a relative. The reference to John Coggins suggests that John Alexander began the seating of the patent before his death; if so the Indian war that supervened put an end to it for the time being. The name Holmes became attached to the northern and southern ends of the patent. Alexander's Island was originally called Holmes Island and was still so called as late as 1761. The principal affluent of Great Hunting Creek bears the name of Holmes Run, after John Holmes who located in the neighborhood in the late seventeenth century.

The patent was first surveyed on February 26–1694 by Theodorick Bland, surveyor of Stafford County. No copy survives but the record of a suit in the Fairfax County Court contains a recital that it was produced before Daniel Jennings, Surveyor of Fairfax in 1746. [5] The way in which Bland laid off the tract is indicated by Jennings' report. The last course of the patent ran east 720 poles. Bland reversed this course, which carried the northwest corner of the patent two miles inland to a point between the present villages of Clarendon and Ballston. He then fixed the pokecory tree 520 poles up Hunting Creek at the southwest corner of the patent, and ran a line, with blazed trees north 15 degrees west to connect them marking the northwest corner with three notches. The area so enclosed comprised 8438 acres, according to Jenning's computation. No grants west of the Howsing patent had been made in 1694. There was no one to challenge the legitimacy of this north 15 degrees west line except the agent of the Proprietor of the Northern Neck, who was not apprized; but it was to lead to prolonged litigation which in one suit after another lasted half a century. If Bland had run the west line north 6 degrees west, he would have enclosed 6000 acres, and there would have been no litigation.

---

[5] First Fairfax Survey Book 1742–57 pages 11, 12.

In February 1693 Philip Alexander reconveyed to his brother Robert his half interest in the patent, reserving to himself 500 acres in severalty. This Philip married Sarah Ashton, only daughter of Col. John Ashton of Chatterton and died leaving a son, Philip to whom the 500 acres descended. [6] It was located at the junction of the river and Hunting Creek, at the southeast corner of the patent and is shown on a survey of 1741 (facing page 10) as "Philip Alexander's land, 500 acres". He had quarters there in 1741.

In 1687 Robert Alexander deeded to Robert Pimmitt 150 acres on the north bank of Four Mile Run at its junction

---

[6] As this paper does not deal further with this branch of the family, the available information as to its connection with the patent is given in this note. The elder Philip also left three daughters, Jane who married Francis Dade, Elizabeth who married Townsend Dade and Sarah who married Cadwallader Dade. The younger Philip of the text (1704–53) is probably the member of the family from whom Alexandria took its name; as part of his 500 acres was taken for the site of the original town in 1749. He was named one of its trustees, but continued to live at Salisbury in Stafford County. He married Sarah Hooe of "Barnesfield", and left issue, among whom were John, Philip (killed in an affray in 1783—see Life of Mason: Rowland 2–36) Jane, who married Henry Ashton and Col. William Alexander (1744–1814) whose seat was at "Effingham", Prince William County. John Alexander (1736–1776) succeeded his father in the ownership of the tract and the unsold lots in Alexandria. This John Alexander by will dated May 1st, 1775, proved in Stafford County, devised the tract to this infant son William Thornton Alexander. The will named executors and authorized them to lay off lots out of the tract contiguous to Alexandria and convey them, reserving ground rents to William Thornton Alexander. The Fairfax deed books show a number of such conveyances, by the executors and by William Thornton Alexander after attaining his majority. Finally in 1807, William Thornton Alexander conveyed all his interest in the tract and the ground rents to John Taliaferro (Arlington Co. D. B., 5–88). This ended the connection of this branch of the Alexander family with the Howsing patent.

with Potomac. The deed was recorded in one of the lost Stafford deed books, but its existence is otherwise attested.

There is no surviving record to show what use Robert Alexander made of the Howsing tract. He certainly did not live there. As it was probably in his time that the names "Holmes" and "Pearson" were given to two islands included in the tract, it may be that John Holmes and Thomas Pearson occupied them as his tenants. His will styles the land his "plantation" so it is likely he had tenants on the ground. He was a justice of the Stafford Court and died in 1704. His wife's name was Frances. Her maiden name is not known. His will dated December 7th, 1703 devised to his sons, Robert and Charles in fee his plantation on the upper side of Great Hunting Creek. Charles Alexander died intestate and without issue, and the sole ownership of the plantation became vested in Robert Alexander, the second. He was born in 1688 and died in 1735. He married Anne Fowke, daughter of Col. Gerard Fowke of Maryland. Like his father and grandfather he lived on the home plantation at Caledon.

It was during the years of his ownership from 1704 to 1735 that the lands to the west of the Howsing patent passed into private ownership. That was a grant from the Crown, but before the close of the seventeenth century, Lord Culpeper had established his claim to the ownership of the Northern Neck of Virginia, and the grants now to be mentioned were by the agents of his successors.

The procedure in obtaining a patent at this time appears to have been that the applicant selected his tract; ascertained as best he could that it was waste ungranted land; that is, that it did not lie within the bounds of any prior proprietary grant; then made his application to the office of the proprietor's agent for a warrant to have it surveyed. The warrant and survey were returned to the proprietor's office. An initial payment, called a composition, was made, and a patent issued describing the land by metes and bounds. This was delivered to the applicant, and a copy recorded in the land grant book in the proprietary office. A yearly quit rent of two shillings per hundred acres, was stipulated in the patent, failure to pay which worked a forfeiture. The grantee could if he chose, record his patent in the office of the clerk of the county in which the land lay. The grant, however, contained no warranty. If it included land previously granted to another, the Proprietor incurred no responsibility, other than the obligation to refund the composition money. It was the business of the applicant to see that his grant did not conflict with any prior grant, whether by the king or the proprietor.

The proprietary grants of land bordering the west line of the Howsing patent from south to north were:

1. Simon Pearson, 213 acres on the Timber Branch of Hunting Creek dated Feby 19, 1729, [7]

2. Francis Awbrey, 1269 acres north of Pearson, dated February 19, 1729. [8]

3. William Struttfield, 543 acres, dated January 21, 1705. [9]

4. Evans Thomas and Philip Todd, 1215 acres dated August 3d, 1719. [10]

5. James Robertson, two contiguous patents, one for 800 acres dated February 27th, 1729, [11] the other for 629 acres dated March 3d, 1730. [12] Robertson conveyed over

[7] Northern Neck Land Grants (hereinafter called N. N.) C-26.

[8] N. N., C-30. This was an irregular star shaped tract which conflicted with the adjoining patents. The Theological Seminary of Virginia is probably located on it.

[9] N. N., 3-121. This was on the south bank of Four Mile Run extending south toward the Episcopal High School. Its last course ran with the line of Mr. Robert Alexander.

[10] N. N., 5-212. This lay along the north bank of Four Mile Run, extending westwardly about two miles and northerly to the crossing of the Columbia Turnpike and the electric trolley line.

[11] N. N., B-191.

[12] N. N., C-117. These tracts lay north of the Thomas and Todd patent. Their most northerly line passed through the subdivision known as Lyon Park.

7

600 acres off the northerly end of his land; to Simon Pearson, who devised 432 acres of his purchase to his daughter Constantia Chapman, and 195 acres to his daughter Susanna. The Robertson patents had more at stake than the others in the location of the back line of the Howsing patent, as a north 15 degree west course for that line would appropriate a big slice of them. The approximate location of the northerly line of Robertson's patent is shown on Berry's Survey (facing page 10) as "Chapman's Quarter". There were no proprietary grants of land north of that between the north 6 degrees west and the north 15 degrees west line. It was assumed in all these grants that the back line of the Howsing patent was a north and south line.

The Potomac river front north of the Howsing patent was appropriated by other patents.

William Struttfield, 500 acres, Sept. 7th, 1709, [13] a rectangular parcel, fronting on river 130 poles adjoining the north line of the Howsing patent by a depth of 615 poles.

Thomas Houseley or Ouseley, 640 acres on the river above Struttfield. [14]

Thomas Going, 653 acres on the river extending westerly from mouth of Spout run. [15]

Parson James Brechin, 795 acres, December 20, 1713. [16]

---

[13] N. N., 3-227.

[14] The lines of this patent were run by Robert Brooke, surveyor in 1785, as appears by his report in Alexander vs Birch, which describes it as a patent of March 14, 1696 to Thomas Houseley for 640 acres on the Potomac river running up to the mouth of Spout run. I have been unable to find it among the Houseley grants indexed on the Northern Neck land records, but it must have embraced the present Rosslyn.

[15] N. N., 3-204.

[16] N. N., 5-44. Brechin's grant did not reach the river. It included the headwaters of Spout run, and bordered the Going, Houseley and Struttfield patents, north of Ballston and Clarendon.

8

Simon Pearson, 195 acres, February 17, 1729.[17]

James Robertson, 662 acres, January 20, 1724.[18]

These patents account for all, or nearly all, the grants on the river up to the holdings of Thomas Lee at Little Falls.

At a later date George Mason acquired the patents of Struttfield, Houseley and Going (Life of Mason by Rowland 1–118). When the litigation over the boundaries of the Howsing patent began, there was a 75 acre tract opposite Analostan Island, conflicting with the Howsing and Struttfield patents, in the possession of Henry Awbrey, infant heir of Thomas Awbrey. I cannot identify it with any of the Awbrey patents. It may have been acquired from Struttfield. Jenning's survey shows two houses on it, "Capt. Awbrey's house" and "the house where Mary Awbrey, widow of John Awbrey now does live". The part of this tract not lost in the litigation with the Alexanders, was subsequently incorporated in the holdings of George Mason, who succeeded Awbrey in the ferry over the Potomac opposite Rock Creek. The Awbreys soon vanished from the neighborhood, but the early road leading from the ferry to the Falls Church (the precurser of Wilson Boulevard) was still called Awbrey's Road in the early 19th century (See 2nd Fairfax Survey Book page 61).

During Robert Alexander's ownership of the Howsing tract, settlement of this region proceeded apace. His sons, John and Gerard, came up the river. John occupied Pearson's island and Gerard built a house on Holmes island. Richard Wheeler and William Griffin, tenants of Alexander, had a plantation on the river at the north end of the tract opposite Analostan Island. "Mr. Chapman" occupied the river front north of Four Mile Run. Hugh West

[17] This tract was near the Potomac River, about a mile above Spout run. It is recited to adjoin the lands of Parson Brechin, Thomas Going and Col. Mason. It is recorded in N. N., C–28.

[18] Robertson's patent began on the Potomac about a mile below the mouth of Pimmitt run and extended down the river. It is in N. N., C–117.

established his Hunting Creek warehouse on the site of the future Alexandria. The road from the ford over Hunting Creek at Cameron Mill was extended north to connect with Awbrey's ferry. It crossed Four Mile Run where the back line of the Howsing patent crossed, if the back line was run north six degrees west. One Chubb, a tenant of Robert Alexander, established a mill there. It is mentioned in the Todd and Thomas Patent of 1719. After Alexandria and Georgetown became towns the road connecting them made a junction with this road at the crossing of Four Mile Run. South of the run lived Joseph Dasey on Francis Awbrey's patent.

North of Chubb, and on the north bank of Four Mile Run was the tract occupied by Evans Thomas, and by his widow and children, after his death. [19] Further up Four Mile Run, but not on land in controversy, lived the pioneer

---

[19] As stated, this land was patented to Evans Thomas and John Todd in 1719. In 1738 John Todd who had removed to Bath County, North Carolina, conveyed his half interest to John Awbrey of Prince William County. A copy of the deed is in Alexander vs Birch. Evans Thomas remained on the land and apparently assumed to own it to the exclusion of his co-tenant, as the will of John Awbrey made in 1743 and proved in 1744 (Fairfax Wills A–60) directs his executors to renew his "suit against Thomas' heirs as soon as they possibly can, and to spare no cost to defend any ejectment that may hereafter be brought by Alexander". Moses Ball in his deposition in Carlyle vs Alexander taken in 1767 stated that Evans Thomas settled on Four Mile Run and devised his land there to his wife and children, who lived there until they sold to Hugh West for the use of Nathaniel Chapman. There is no will of Evans Thomas in Prince William or Fairfax. The Evans Thomas whose will was the first probated in Loudoun (1757) was probably a son of the Evans Thomas named above. The record does not show whether Awbrey's executor recovered this half interest. In the subsequent suit with the Alexanders, Col. John Carlyle appears as contesting the Alexander claim to the land adjoining Four Mile Run on the north. He may have bought the Awbrey interest, and possibly Chapman's also.

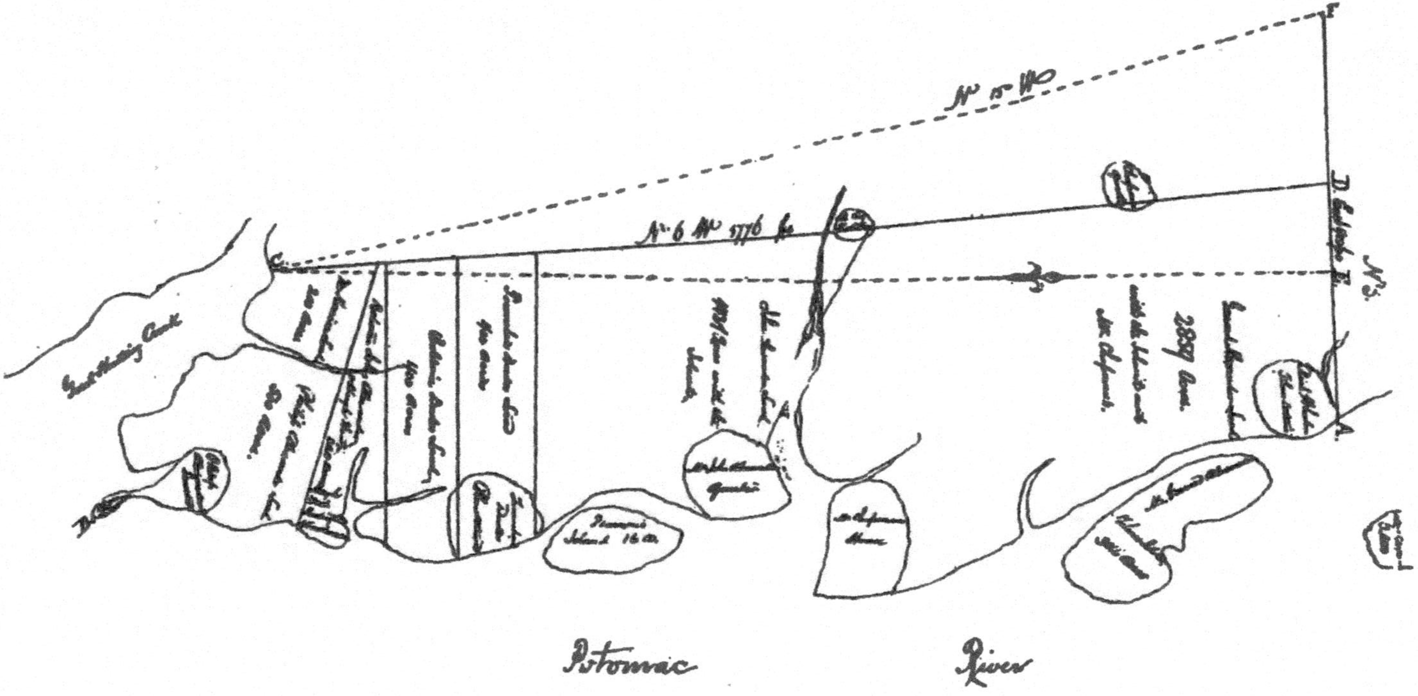
Potomac
River

physician of the neighborhood, Dr. Dangill, according to Moses Ball's statement in Alexander vs Birch. Doctor's Run was evidently named from him.

Robert Alexander died in 1735. His will made in the same year was proved in Stafford County. It gave to his son John "the island in Prince William County, called Pearson's Island where he now lives"; to his daughter Parthenia Massey 400 acres in Prince William; to his son "Gerrard, the island in Prince William commonly called Holms Island, where he now lives"; also 1125 acres adjoining the said island; to his daughter Sarah Alexander 400 acres adjoining Parthenia Massey, the same length on the back line, and the same breadth on the river. All these tracts are described as having negroes and stock on them. All the remainder of his real estate in Prince William to be equally divided between his two sons and their heirs, and he directed that all said land should be entailed "from heir to heir".

Parthenia Massey was the wife of Dade Massey, by whom she had a son, Lee Massey (1732–1814), the well known minister of Pohick Church.[20] Becoming a widow Parthenia Massey married Townsend Dade. Sarah Alexander married Baldwin Dade, his brother. Robert Alexander appears to have conveyed in his lifetime 220 acres to Hugh West and John Alexander. This was situated at the south end of his tract next to Philip Alexander's 500 acres. Part of it was incorporated into the town of Alexandria. Robert Alexander's will indicated generally the location of the tracts devised. The divisees made the actual division of the land among themselves and for this purpose caused the whole tract to be surveyed by Joseph Berry. A

---

[20] Lee Massey was the grandson of John Massey who was in the present Fairfax County in 1734. He was a descendant of the Rev. Lee Massey of St. Mary's County, Md. an early minister of St. George's Church, Poplar Hill, where his tombstone may still be seen. Lee Massey of the text had his seat in his later years on Belmont Bay at the mouth of Occoquan.

reproduction of his survey faces page 10. It bears this Legend: "Surveyed for Messrs. John and Gerard Alexander and others, 6000 acres of land in Prince William County on the freshes of the Potomac River, beginning at A, an old red oak standing at the mouth of a small branch near opposite to an island formerly called My Lord's Island, and running down the several courses of the Potomac River, crossing several creeks to a marked hickory at B, the south-eastermost point of Great Hunting Creek; thence up the several courses of Hunting Creek to C the root of an old hickory, being an ancient corner of said tract; thence north 6 degrees West 1776 poles to D; thence east 410 poles to the beginning. The dotted line C. E. is north and south mentioned in the patent, but does not give the quantity by 933 acres; the dotted line C. F. is north 15 degrees west which is according to an ancient survey of William Blans and gives the last course 720 poles to the beginning, according to the patent. All the several divisions are described by black lines, and every person claiming within his own plat.

Surveyed and divided between the parties as described in the plat in part of the first and second weeks in April 1741. Joseph Berry".

"William Blans" is a mistake for Theodorick Bland. The name is correctly given in Daniel Jennings' survey in 1746 of the same tract recorded at page 11 of the earliest Fairfax survey book.

The Berry plat, however, shows a strange omission. All the land north of Four Mile Run is assigned to Gerard Alexander, but 150 acres on the north bank of the run did not belong to the Alexanders. As stated, the first Robert Alexander had deeded it to John Pimmitt in 1687 and in 1741 the Chapman family was in possession, claiming under that deed.[11] The plat shows "Mr. Chapman's house" as if he were a tenant.

---

[11] John Pimmitt's son and heir, George Pimmitt in 1707 conveyed this 150 acres to William Harper describing it by metes and bounds which agree with subsequent surveys of the Chapman tract. (Stafford D. B.,

Robert Alexander's will passed title to 4930 acres of the original tract. It gave 800 acres to his two daughters; Pearson's Island (16 acres) to his son John: Holmes Island (302 acres) and 1125 acres adjoining to his son Gerard. This left about 2500 acres to be divided between John and Gerard. The course of Four Mile Run suggested a convenient division. John Alexander took his dividend to the south of it, and Gerard to the north. The land between the north 6 degrees west line and the north 15 degrees west line, was not assigned, and such claim to it as Robert Alexander had remained in John and Gerard. John was the older son and was compensated for the smaller part of the patent given to him, by a devise of land in Stafford. All lands passing by the will were entailed "from heir to heir".

John Alexander was born in 1711 and died in 1764. He married Susanna, daughter of Capt. Simon Pearson of Stafford on December 11, 1734. How long after his marriage he continued to live on Pearson's Island is not known; apparently not long, as he is usually styled John Alexander of Chotank. A recital in a deed from Townsend Dade to him in 1745 styles him "of Stafford" and in his will made in 1763 he calls himself a resident of St. Paul's parish in

Z–403). John Withers Harper, heir of Willam Harper conveyed the same tract in 1732 to Thomas Pearson (Prince William D. B., B–1). Pearson's sister Constantia married Nathaniel Chapman. There is no known record of a deed from Pearson, but there can be no doubt that in 1741 a Chapman, either Nathaniel or his father, Jonathan, was in possession of this land claiming to own it, under a deed or a transfer of possession from Thomas Pearson. There was subsequent litigation between Gerard Alexander and Nathaniel Chapman, but it was over the location of the dividing lines between them. The house subsequently known as Abingdon was built by Gerard Alexander about this time. It passed later to John Parke Custis who gave it the name of Abingdon. The Alexander and Chapman homes (the latter called Summer Hill) were the first houses of any consequence on the river north of Four Mile Run. It does not appear that the Alexanders ever gave the Howsing patent a tract name.

13

Stafford. His will was proved there in 1764. He probably went back to live at Caledon after the death of his mother. His widow returned to Fairfax. His children were Charles (1737–1806), Simon, John, born 1739, Thomas Pearson, William Pearson, Robert, Susanna, Elizabeth and Ann who married Charles Binns, most of whom were residents of Fairfax.

Gerard Alexander spent his life on the land assigned to him in the partition of his father's estate, living in the house subsequently called Abingdon. He was one of the original trustees of the town of Alexandria; a burgess from Fairfax from 1751 to 1755, and was known as Col. Gerard Alexander. His will was proved in Fairfax in 1761. His descendants will be mentioned later.

The practice of entailing land was common and on the increase in Virginia when Robert Alexander died, but John and Gerard Alexander determined to break the entail and acquire the absolute ownership of their tracts. Accordingly in 1742 they sued out from the office of the Secretary of the Province a writ ad quod damnum addressed to the Sheriff of Fairfax to determine whether they might sell 4249 acres in Truro Parish.[22] An inquisition was had and

---

[22] Virginia legislation of the early eighteenth century favored the entailing of land, by which it could be kept in the same family for generations. The acts of Assembly of 1705 and 1710 forbade the docking of entails by fine and recovery, which were fictitious suits in use in England, to enable the owner of entailed land to sell it. Thereafter a private act of the Assembly was necessary to permit a tenant in tail to sell, and such acts required other land of the petitioner held in fee simple to be settled on him in tail upon the same limitations as the land docked. These private acts give much interesting information about the leading families of eighteenth century Virginia. By acts passed in 1734 (4th Hen. 400) and 1748 (5 Hen. 414) the legislature so far departed from its declared policy as to permit small entailed parcels to be sold by the simpler proceeding of a writ and inquisition, such as the Alexanders undertook to avail themselves of. The preamble to the act of 1748 states that many poor people are seised of small parcels,

14

the jury found that His Majesty would suffer no damage if John and Gerard Alexander should sell their lands. The value of the land was fixed at 150 lbs. John and Gerard then conveyed to their brother in law Townsend Dade and he by separate deeds made in 1745 reconveyed to John Alexander 1421 acres in fee simple and to Gerard Alexander 2713 acres in fee simple. [23]

The Berry plat, however, shows the land north of Four Mile Run which had been assigned to Gerard Alexander as containing 2859 acres, a discrepancy of about 140 acres, due to failure to exclude the Chapman parcel of 150 acres from the land assigned to Gerard.

The inquisition proceeding purporting to dock the entail was a palpable subterfuge. The land was of much greater value than 200 pounds. Townsend Dade was not a purchaser, but a conduit of title. The proceeding could doubtless have been set aside at the instance of the heirs in tail of either John or Gerard Alexander. Realizing this,

---

often ignorantly and undesignedly by their ancestors devised in tail, and the docking of such entails by easier methods will be a great relief to such persons, who must be confined to labor upon such parcels, when by selling them, they might be enabled to purchase slaves and other lands more improvable. The method provided by both acts allowed any person seised in tail of lands not exceeding two hundred pounds sterling in value and not contiguous to other lands held by him in tail, to sue out a writ ad quod damnum from the office of the Secretary of the Colony, addressed to the sheriff of the County in which the land lay, commanding him to summon a jury to value the land and to ascertain whether it was a separate tract not adjoining other entailed land of the same person, and not of a value exceeding two hundred pounds; and if the jury so found, its verdict, with a survey of the land, was returned to the office of the Secretary, and the tenant in tail was then authorized to sell to a bona fide purchaser, by a deed recorded in the General Court of the Colony, discharged from the entail. The whole system of entails was swept away by the Jeffersonian legislation of 1776.

[23] Copies of the deeds from Townsend Dade are a part of the record in Alexander vs Birch.

Gerard Alexander in 1753 procured an Act of the General Assembly of Virginia, [24] docking the entail as to 2713 acres held by him and settling other land of his in Frederick County and the present Loudoun County on him as tenant in tail. The previous attempt to dock the entail by the inquisition was not mentioned in the act. Its invalidity was assumed. John Alexander made no effort to secure the passage of a similar act. Shortly before his death he deeded to eldest son, Charles, the land that the inquisition had supposedly freed from the entail. Charles Alexander had therefore no interest in questioning the regularity of the proceeding and after 1776 the whole matter became academic.

John Alexander, it seems, attempted to dissuade or prevent his brother Gerard from procuring the Act of Assembly docking the entail. The testimony in the subsequent suit of Alexander vs Birch ranged over much extraneous matter. Parson Lee Massey, the cousin of John and Gerard Alexander, was a witness, and stated that he had heard that Gerard Alexander attempted to dock the entail in Great Britain and was opposed by John Alexander. On cross examination this colloquy took place.

"Q. Was not Gerard Alexander in possession back to the north 17 degree west line when he attempted to dock the entail in Great Britain? A. Can't say.

Q. Did not John Alexander enter a caveat in Great Britain against docking said entail?

A. John and Gerard told him so. Gerard complained of his brother's conduct.

Q. Was not Gerard Alexander aways apprehensive that if a line further west than the north six degrees west line should be established he would lose some of his riverside land and his dwelling house?

A. Yes."

The apprehension of Gerard Alexander is comprehensible, but the reference to a caveat in Great Britain is mys-

---

[24] Henning's Statutes, 6-399.

tifying to the present writer. It is true that the Crown could disallow any act of the colonial assembly and occasionally did so, when it deemed that the profits of British merchants might be diminished by proposed colonial legislation. But it was hardly conceivable that a private act docking an entail should be vetoed in England at the instance of a person in Virginia who objected to it. Such a precedent would have raised an uproar in Virginia.

Neither the ad quod damnum of John and Gerard Alexander nor the private act docking the entail of Gerard Alexander's land affected the land lying between the north 6 degrees west line and the north 15 degrees west line containing nearly 2500 acres. That land, or rather, the Alexander claim to it remained undivided·in the two brothers in tail, but much the larger portion of it lay west of the land assigned to Gerard Alexander in severalty. If the land should be adjudged a part of the Howsing patent, a redrawing of the boundary between John and Gerard might be demanded by John, with the possible result of depriving Gerard of the south part of his river front and his dwelling house. This is the probable reason why he took little part in the ensuing litigation over the western line though in the end his heirs benefited by the victory of John Alexander's son Charles. It was also the fact that the southerly part of the contested land was more valuable, because nearer Alexandria.

SUITS OVER THE BOUNDARY
OF THE HOWSING PATENT

When Fairfax County was formed in 1742, civil justice in Virginia was administered by county courts in the first instance, with appellate jurisdicton in the General Court of the Colony. The justices of the county courts were appointed by the Governor with the consent of the Council, from among the "most able, honest and judicious" citizens of the county, and subsequent vacancies were filled in the same way.   They were not lawyers, but were usually chosen from the principal land owners of the county.   The commission appointing the justices named certain of them, not less than four, as the quorum and no valid court be held without the presence of one of the quorum.   The jurisdiction of the court resembled the combined jurisdiction of the principal courts of England, and trial by jury could be demanded in any case in which a jury trial was accorded by the common law.   At least four courts a year were required to be held in Fairfax by Act of Assembly. [25]   No doubt more frequent courts were held as the population of the county increased.

The General Court was held at Williamsburg and was composed of the Governor and the whole body of the Council.   While not lawyers, the councilors were men of wealth, accustomed to the management of important business. The greater number of them had been justices of the county courts, before being appointed to the Council and had acquired there some knowledge of legal procedure.

The Council was also the upper house of the Colonial Assembly, but its legislative and judicial functions were exercised separately.   In the restored Capitol at Williamsburg, the council chamber is on the second floor, with accommodations for its members only.   The General Court chamber is a larger room on the first floor.   A raised gallery for the judges extends across the back of the room.   Desks and tables for attorneys are in front of it, with benches for witnesses and spectators, and a small gallery is built into the east wall.

The first of the suits over the boundaries of the Howsing patent appears to have been an ejectment brought by John and Gerard Alexander about 1742 through their fictitious tenant Aminidab Thrustout against a feigned defendant whose designation has not survived.   The actual defendant was Henry Awbrey, infant son and heir of Thomas Awbrey.   The land in dispute was a triangular parcel

---

[25] 6 Henning 201.

18

along the Potomac River containing 33 acres. The source of Awbrey's title does not appear. It conflicted with the Howsing patent, unless the northerly line of that patent could be pushed further down the river to the branch next south of Wampakan Branch. The only surviving record of the suit is the survey made by Daniel Jennings Surveyor of Fairfax County on March 31, 1746 in obedience to the Order of the General Court. Annexed to the survey is his report recorded in the first Fairfax Survey Book p 11. The land in controversy was far away from the western line of the Howsing patent, but it was deemed necessary to lay off the whole patent. The report states that the plaintiffs produced an attested copy of the patent to Howsing for 6000 acres and a survey and plat of Theod. Bland, Surveyor of Stafford Co. dated Feby. 26th, 1693–94. A witness pointed out to Jennings the beginning point on the Potomac River opposite My Lords Island, at the mouth of Wampakan Branch and the plaintiffs required him to reverse the last course of the patent by running west 720 poles to a point over two miles inland, fixing the supposed northwest corner of the patent. The parties then took themselves to a spot in the north side of Hunting Creek where a witness, Thomas West, showed Jennings a rotten hickory stump said to be the southwest corner of the Howsing patent. The plaintiffs then required the surveyor to connect these two points by a north 15$\frac{1}{2}$ degrees west line. The patent as thus outlined contained 8438 acres. The records of the General Court at the old Capitol and of the County Court of Fairfax showing further proceedings in this suit are missing but the report of Robert Brooke, Surveyor, in the later suit of Alexander vs Birch made in the year 1785 [26] states that the plaintiffs in the later suit required that the 3d line of the survey be run North 18$\frac{3}{4}$ degrees West 1915 poles, which line, the plaintiffs state, are the bounds of the Howsing patent as fixed at a General Court at the Capitol November 1751 on trial of a suit by John and Gerard Alexander

[26] The surveyor's report covers pages 101 to 119 of the Land Suit Book No. 1.

against Awbrey and others. So it appears that the Alexanders won their suit against Awbrey. Awbrey, however, was not concerned over the location of the westerly line of the Howsing patent as the land he occupied was on the river two miles away. But there were others who were vitally interested in the location of that line. Moses Ball testifying in 1767 in a later suit [27] stated that he never heard the Alexanders claimed any land beyond their westerly north 6 degrees west line until the dispute with Awbrey and that no persons before that who lived west of that line acknowledged themselves tenants of the Alexanders.

During the litigation over the westerly line, the adjoining tracts were owned as follows:

1. Simon Pearson's Timber Branch patent by his daughter Margaret, who married successively William Henry Terrett and Col. John West. There is no surviving record of litigation over this land.

2. Francis Awbrey's 1261 acre patent. [28] This was

---

[27] Alexander vs Birch where Moses Ball's deposition in an earlier suit was put in evidence.

[28] Francis Awbrey's will (Prince William Wills, C–341) devised to his son Richard a half of his tract on Four Mile Run adjoining the land of Alexander and to his son Henry the other half of that tract. Richard Awbrey's will, recorded in the Fairfax Wills Book A page 79, made no disposition of his half interest. John Awbrey his oldest brother seems to have claimed it by descent. His will (Fairfax Wills A–60) devised the tract of land "falling to me by the death of Richard Awbrey, lying on Four Mile Run where Joseph Dasey now lives and containing 630½ acres to be equally divided between my wife's two daughters Hannah and Frances". By two deeds (copies filed in Alexander vs Birch) Owen Brady and wife Hanover of St. Marys Co., Md., and Frances Awbrey each conveyed to John Carlyle a moiety of the land on Four Mile Run devised by the will of John Awbrey. The deeds are dated May 1, 1763. By an earlier deed dated March 7, 1749 (copy recorded in Alexander vs Birch) Henry Awbrey conveyed all his interest in the tract of 1261 acres patented by Francis Awbrey to William Ramsay. Francis and Thomas Awbrey also joined in the same deed, though why they joined is not explained.

owned by William Ramsay[29] and John Carlyle both of Alexandria. It was an irregularly shaped patent conflicting with the north 15 degrees west line claimed for the Howsing patent, and also with Pearson and Struttfield.[30] A tongue of it projected north across Four Mile Run.

3.   Struttfield's 543 acre patent on the south bank of Four Mile Run. In 1756 John Carlyle became its owner, though the legal title was not gotten until after his death.[31]

4.   On the north bank of the run was the Thomas and Todd patent owned by John Carlyle or Nathaniel Chapman; it is not certain which.

5.   North of Thomas and Todd lay James Robertson's tracts. He died in 1769 and was succeeded by his son John and his daughter Janet Birch.

6.   North of Robertson was the land he had sold to Simon Pearson, and willed by the latter to his daughters, Susanna Alexander and Constantia Chapman.

The Alexanders filed suit in 1743, an ejectment against Robertson. No record of the suit survives. The opinion of the Court of Appeals of Virginia in a later suit[32] states this was begun in 1743 by John Alexander, and that he recovered judgment in 1751 for so much of Robertson's land as was included in the Howsing patent. This judgment did not conclude the adjoining proprietors, and while the suit was still in progress, William Ramsey took the offen-

---

[29] William Ramsay was a native of Scotland who settled at Alexandria before 1749. He was one of the original trustees of that town. He died in 1785 and is buried in the grave yard of Christ Church. He was the original purchaser of lots 46 and 47 at the intersection of King and Fairfax streets, on which he built in 1752 the frame house still standing which is claimed to be and probably is the oldest house in Alexandria. His son, Col. Dennis Ramsay, was a pall bearer at Washington's funeral.

[30] A survey by George West, Surveyor of Fairfax, recorded in First Fairfax S. B. page 36 shows these overlaps.

[31] For further particulars on the struttfield patent, see page 10'.

[32] 1st Washington's Virginia Reports page 34 Alexander vs. Birch.

21

sive with a suit against John Alexander. As his suit was in trespass Ramsey's object could be obtained by a verdict against either of the Alexanders. Here again the records are missing, but a copy of the judgment of the General Court at Williamsburg on October 25th, 1758 adjudging that the defendant Alexander was guilty of trespass, was introduced in evidence in the later suit of John Carlyle vs Alexander and again in the suit of Alexander vs Birch.[33] This put a check to the Alexanders' pretentions, and both Robertson and John Carlyle started suits in ejectment. Both were successful. The same opinion of the Court of Appeals referred to states "that James Robertson recovered from Robert Alexander and was put in possession of the lands contained within his grant by writ of possession in 1765". John Alexander had died the year before. Robert was one of his sons. The land that Robertson got back was the same he had lost in his prior suit. The only surviving record of the record suit between Robertson[34] and the Alexanders is the report to the Fairfax County Court by the county surveyor, of his survey of Robertson's patent. Its beginning point at a white oak standing on the Southeast side of the back road along Long Branch was located by Moses Ball. Robertson was represented by the well known Alexandria attorney, George Johnson.[35]

---

[33] 1st Fairfax Survey Book pages 60 & 61; also Alexander vs Birch.

[34] James Robertson died in 1769. His will recorded in Fairfax Wills Book C page 47 is dated Sept. 4th, 1760 and was made while his second suit was in progress. He gave personalty to his wife Elizabeth; to his son John the tract, "I now live on consisting of 630 acres, except in case the Alexanders should obtain that tract adjoining Todd and Evans", then his daughter Janet should have 320 acres of it; to his daughter Janet Baumaker Robertson the tract adjoining Todd and Thomas' 630 acres; to his god daughter Elizabeth, the daughter of John Robertson 100 acres on Four Mile Run; the residue of the estate was devised to son James Robertson.

[35] George Johnson came to Virginia from Scotland before 1748, and soon became one of the most prominent lawyers in northern Virginia.

John Carlyle also sued the Alexanders. In 1767 a survey was made pursuant to order of the General Court in the ejectment of John Carlyle vs Charles Alexander. The record in Alexander vs Birch contains a copy of the decree of that court dated May 4th, 1771, declaring that the defendant Charles Alexander was guilty of trespass; and a deposition of Moses Ball taken in 1767 on behalf of Carlyle. It is difficult to determine just what parcels were involved in this litigation. Carlyle owned a half interest in the Francis Awbrey patent, also the whole of the Struttfield patent, a corner of which lay within the extreme line of the Alexander claim. The only surviving deposition (that of Ball) indicates that a part of the Thomas and Todd patent on the north bank of Four Mile Run, was also in controversy. If so Carlyle must have bought out either Chapman or Awbrey's executor or both. Throughout his life in Virginia, Carlyle was a persistent purchaser of land, chiefly in Fairfax County. At his death he probably owned as much land in the county as did Washington. The same Fairfax survey book[36] shows another suit in progress at this time in which Col. Gerard Alexander sued Nathaniel Chapman "in ejection" but the matter in controversy appears to have been the bounds of the 150 acres on the Potomac river north of Four Mile Run owned by Chapman.

The records of the General Court were destroyed in 1865. Manuscript notes of some of its decisions have been preserved and were published some years ago. The published decisions contain no cases later than 1743. It is not

He represented Fairfax County in the House of Burgesses for some years. It is said Jefferson gave him the credit for drafting Patrick Henry's Stamp Act resolution of 1765. He had a house in Alexandria and a country estate, "Belvale", on the present Telegraph Road about four miles southwest of Alexandria. He married a daughter of Dennis McCarthy, and died shortly before 1770. He left sons William (1752–1815) and George. The latter was an aide de camp to Washington in the Revolutionary War.

[36] First Fairfax S. B. 39–63. For the Chapman family see page 81.

possible therefore, to assign the reasons which led the court to decide the two earlier cases of Awbrey and Robertson in favor of the north 15 degree west line claimed by the Alexanders, and subsequently against this claim up to that line in the later suits of Ramsey, Carlyle and Robertson. The controversy died down and was not revived until the Revolutionary War ended; by which time the original antagonists were mostly dead.

COL. GERARD ALEXANDER'S ESTATE

Col. Gerard (or Gerrard) Alexander died in 1761, the owner of all the Howsing patent north of Four Mile Run and east of the north 6 degree west boundary of that patent except the part belonging to Chapman, and co-owner with his brother John of the claim to the contested strip west of that. He left a widow Mary, four sons Robert, Philip, George and Gerrard and daughters Nancy and Mary Ann. Having docked the entail he was free to devise his land, which he did.[37] To his son Robert he gave "the house where in I now live and 904 acres adjoining it"; to his son Philip "904 acres formerly leased to Robert Osborn with the island therein included known the name of Homes Island"; to his son Gerard "900 acres of the upper part of the tract whereon I now live". These devises comprised all the Howsing patent north of Four Mile Run owned by the testator exclusive of the contested area. The residue of his estate was given to the four sons, Robert, Philip, George and Gerard. The three sons Robert, Philip and Gerard, went into possession of the tracts given them by the will, but did not mark the division lines between them by survey. Robert took the southern, Philip the middle, and Gerard the northern part of the tract. Many years later, in the settlement of a controversy between the estate of John Parke Custis, and the Alexanders, such a survey was made to fix these boundaries.[38]

---

[37] Fairfax Wills, 7–327.
[38] 2nd Fairfax Co. Survey Book (1787–1856) p 61.

24

John Parke Custis (1753–1781) was the son of Martha Dandridge Custis, and the stepson of George Washington. His father, Daniel Parke Custis, was an extensive tobacco planter and lived at the "White House" on the Pamunkey River in New Kent County. He died in 1757[39] at the age of 45, leaving a large estate to his widow and two children John Parke and Martha Parke Custis. On January 6, 1759 the widow became the wife of Col. George Washington. The wedding ceremony took place at the White House, and after a honeymoon of three months, the couple with the two children took up their residence at Mt. Vernon. Washington assumed the management of the Custis estate and the guardianship of the two children. Martha Parke Custis ("Patsey") died in an epileptic fit in 1773. A tutor was employed for John at Mt. Vernon, but he proved an indolent scholar. "His mind", Washington wrote, "is more turned to dogs, horses and guns, and indeed upon dress and equipage". He was next put under the care and tuition of the Rev. Jonathan Boucher at Annapolis, where he lived for three years. During this time he engaged himself to Eleanor Calvert, daughter of Bendict Calvert of Mt. Airy, Prince George County, Maryland, without the knowledge of his mother or of Washington. The match was one to which no exception could be taken on the score

---

[39] The Custis line runs (1) John born in Gloucestershire; kept an English tavern in Rotterdam, emigrated to Virginia about 1640, settled in Northampton County on the eastern shore. (2) Col. John of Arlington, Northampton (1630–1696), member of the Council of Virginia; married a daughter of Col. Edmund Searborough; was commissioned a major general by Gov. Berkeley after his flight to the Eastern Shore. (3) John (1653–1713), member of the Council 1699. (4) John (1680–1750) member of the Council 1727; married Frances, daughter of Col. John Parke. The story of his domestic infelicity and of his having it recounted on his tombstone is well known. (5) Daniel Parke Custis of the text.

either of the young woman's character or family. Washington feared that the engagement might "precipitate him into a marriage before, I am certain, he has ever bestowed a serious thought of the consequences", and took young Custis to New York, where he put him in King's College. Shortly after, Patsy Custis died, and her brother returned to Mt. Vernon and married. He and his wife lived for several years at the "White House" in King William and there the two older children of the marriage, Eliza and Martha, were presumably born. Custis owned several large plantations in New Kent and King William and a house in Williamsburg. Both husband and wife were anxious to come back to the neighborhood of Mt. Vernon and Mt. Airy. In 1778 Custis entered into negotiations with Gerard and Robert Alexander to buy their plantations on the Potomac above Four Mile Run. He must have written to Washington about it, for the latter wrote to Custis in May of that year:

"With respect to your purchase of Mr. Robert Alexander I can only say that the price you have offered for it is a very great one, but as you want it to live at and it answers yours and Nellie's views and is a pleasant seat and capable of great improvement, I do not think the price ought to be a capital object with you".[40]

Washington had fox hunted with Robert Alexander dozens of times and knew him well enough to predict that Custis would be no match for him in a bargain. On July 15, 1778 in a letter from the White House Custis told Washington of the terms of his purchase.

"Besides the extravagancy of the price it (the contract) is a disagreeable one. Nothing could have induced me to have given such terms but the inconquerable desire I have to live in the neighborhood of Mt. Vernon and in the County of Fairfax. I have agreed to give him (Robert Alexander) 12 pounds per acre, and at the expiration of 24 years to pay him the principal with compound interest.

---

[40] Fitspatrick's Writings of Washington, 11–457.

26

This is a hard and disagreeable article. ... I have agreed to give Gerard 11 pounds per acre, the money to be paid at Christmas. The reason that induced me to purchase his land was the advantage of having my estate under my own eye and the probability of getting Phil's which I understand he wants to sell. If I should get his, my tract would be very complete and good in Quality, situate in a part of the state where lands will rise in value."[41] Custis wanted the Philip Alexander tract because it lay between his purchases from Robert and Gerard Alexander. He never got it.

Washington was dumfounded when he learned the conditions of Custis' bargain with Robert Alexander, and he wrote from his camp at White Plains:

"As a friend and one who has your welfare at heart, let me entreat you to consider the consequences of paying compound interest. Your having 24 years to pay Mr. Robt. Alexander without his having it in his power to call upon you for any part of the principal or interest is, in my judgment, an unfortunate circumstance for you. A dun now then might serve as a monitor to remind you of the evil tendency of paying compound interest and the fatal consequence which may result from letting a matter of this sort sleep. Without it you may be plunged into an enormous debt without thinking of it or giving that timely attention which the importance of it is requisite. I presume you are not unacquainted with the fact of 12000 pounds at compound interest amounting to upward of 48000 pounds in twenty-four years. Reason therefore must convince you that unless you avert the evil by a deposit of a like sum in the loan office, and there hold sacred to the purpose of accumulating in the same proportion you pay, that you will have abundant reason to repent it. No Virginia estate (except a few under the best management) can stand simple interest. How then can they bear compound interest!"[42] Washington also thought the 1100 lbs paid Gerard Alexander extravagant.

---

[41] Custis Manuscript Library of Congress.
[42] Writing's of Washington (Ford) p 144.

27

It does not appear whether the contract called for payment of the purchase money in specie or in paper currency which the war had already much depreciated. It is supposed that each deed conveyed 1000 acres. Both deeds were made in December 1778 and recorded in Liber N pages 223 and 226 of the Fairfax Records and Custis gave Robert Alexander a purchase money mortgage. The book is missing. The western boundary of both tracts was the north 6 degrees west line of the Howsing patent, but Custis gave Robert Alexander a bond of the same date to purchase Alexander's land between the north 6 degrees west and the north 15 degrees west line estimated to contain 250 acres. The unexpressed condition of the bond was probably that possession be delivered to Custis.

Custis and his family must have taken immediate possession of Robert Alexander's house, as it is known that Eleanor Parke Custis (Nellie Custis) was born thereon March 21, 1779. The house and estate was thereafter known as Abingdon. Custis entered local politics and was elected a delegate to the legislature from Fairfax. His step father at his camp on the Hudson evidently heard unfavorable reports of his doings at Richmond and lectured him roundly:

"Dear Custis: I do not suppose that so young a senator as you are, so little versed in political disquisitions, can yet have much influence in a popular assembly, composed of variour talents and different views, but it is in your power to be punctual in attendance". [43]

The last surviving letter from Washington to Custis was written from Dobbs Ferry on July 25, 1781 about the mortgage debt to Robert Alexander. In the two and a half years since the purchase of Abingdon, the continental currency had sunk to a nominal value and Custis was contemplating gathering 12000 pounds with compound interest in paper currency and tendering them to Robert Alexander, with an additional allowance to compensate him for the

[43] Writings of Washington (Ford) 9 p 174.

28

intervening depreciation. Washington wrote that Custis' offer was apparently founded "on principles of justice so far as I can form a judgment without seeing the mortgage or having recourse to the original agreement and the missives which passed between you."[44] If the contract permitted payment in paper money Washington thought Alexander would get his deserts by being paid off in paper. Nothing came of the proposal as Custis had but three more months to live. At the siege of Yorktown he served as a volunteer aide de camp on Washington's staff, contracted camp fever and was taken to Eltham where he died.

In a letter to Lafayette from Mt. Vernon Washington wrote:

"On that day (November 5, 1781) I arrived at Eltham (the seat of Col. Bassett) time enough to see poor Mr. Custis breathe his last. This unexpected and affecting event threw Mrs. Washington and Mrs. Custis who were both present into such deep distress that the circumstances of it and a duty I owed to the deceased in assisting at his funeral rites, prevented my reaching this place until the 13th."

There were four children of the marriage; Elizabeth born in 1776, married Thomas Law, the English speculator, who played a considerable part in the development of the "Federal City". The well known Rogers family of Baltimore, donors of Druid Hill Park, descend from this marriage; Martha, born 1777 who married Thomas Peter of Georgetown, builder of Tudor Place, which her descendants still occupy; Eleanor born March 1779 who married Lawrence Lewis, Washington's nephew. They built Woodlawn, on a part of the Mt. Vernon estate overlooking the Washington and Richmond Highway; George Washington Parke Custis, born April 30th, 1781. Washington adopted the two younger children and they were reared at Mt. Vernon. The widow and the two older children returned to Abingdon. In 1783 she married Dr. David Stuart, by whom it is said she had 12 children. The couple resided

---

[44] Writings of Washington (Ford) 9 p 315.

for several years at Abingdon. Before marrying again she seems to have tried to get Washington's views, but he declined to commit himself. "I never did, nor do I believe I ever shall, give advice to a woman who is setting out on a matrimonial voyage; first, because I never could advise one to marry without her consent, and secondly, because I know it is to no purpose to advise her to refrain, when she has obtained it."[45]

Although entails were abolished in Virginia in 1776, the common law canon of descent giving preference to males over females remained in force until 1785, so that on the death of his father, George Washington Parke Custis became the owner of the parts of the Howsing patent purchased by the former. He was still a very young child, and Dr. Stuart had at once to tackle the problem of the Abingdon tract, saddled as it was the debt to Robert Alexander. He was the administrator of John Parke Custis' estate and in bargaining with Alexander, he had the advantage of his possible right to discharge the debt in the now almost worthless continental money. The result of the negotiation is embodied in an Act of the Virginia legislature passed on November 17, 1789 reciting that Alexander had agreed to take back the land upon being paid a reasonable compensation for its use, but that no contract could be made by the infant heir without the interposition of the Assembly. It was thereon enacted that any contract which said Stuart with the written consent of George Washington, should make as to the surrender of the land to Robert Alexander, should be valid.[46] Stuart and Alexander each named two arbitrators and these named a fifth, the Rev. Bryan Fairfax. The arbitrators made an award that Robert Alexander should be paid 70 pounds per hundred acres, annual rent, for the twelve years since Custis' purchase, which was filed at the Court of Fairfax (then in Alexandria).[47] This

---

[45] Ford's Writings of Washington, 10–317.
[46] 13 Hennings Statutes, page 99.
[47] Fairfax D. B., U–257.

was followed by a deed dated October 1, 1792 by Stuart as administrator, acting under the authority of the Act of the Legislature. The thousand acre tract purchased from Gerard Alexander remained the property of the younger Custis. He lived at Mt. Vernon until the death of Martha Washington 1802, when he commenced the building of Arlington mansion. In 1804 he married Mary Lee Fitzhugh, daughter of William Fitzhugh of Ravensworth, and as well known, spent the rest of his long life at Arlington House.

After his sale to John Parke Custis in 1778, Gerard Alexander removed to his lands in Frederick County, Virginia, where his will was proved about 1800. Neither he nor his descendants thereafter claimed to own any land embraced in the Howsing patent.

ALEXANDER VS BIRCH

It would be natural to suppose that the two prior suits between John Alexander and James Robertson had settled the ownership of the land in dispute between them, but the ancient English land law abounded in doctrines strange to modern readers. The action of ejectment in universal use in the eighteenth century as a means of trying title to land was a personal action between the parties and settled nothing but the present right to possession. The General Court of the colony was abolished during the Revolution, and a new system of judicature established. The county courts were retained, but new district courts were set up over them, one being the District Court of Dumfries, and over all was a Court of Appeals at Richmond. Charles Alexander had succeeded to the claim of his father, John, and Janet Birch was the devisee of her father, James Robertson. There was no legal obstacle to prevent Charles Alexander from threshing out the whole controversy again in court; at least, so far as the half interest of John Alexander was concerned, and this he did. The sons of Col. Gerard Alexander took no part in the suit. This appears strange, as the land in controversy was north of Four Mile Run, and directly west of the land assigned to Robert Alexander in the division of Col. Gerard Alexander's estate. The Abingdon tract up to the north 6 degrees west line, at this time belonged to the infant heir of John Parke Custis, but there was a recorded contract binding Custis to purchase any additional land adjoining Abingdon west of the north 6 degrees west line that Robert Alexander might recover. As Robert Alexander was then in controversy with the Custis estate, he may not have cared to embark in more law suits. By the time he settled his controversy with Dr. Stuart and had gotten back his land, Alexander vs. Birch had been decided.

A suit in ejectment at this time was based on a pretended lease by a fictitious plaintiff to a fictitious defendant. The usual antagonists were John Doe and Richard Roŵe, but the custom in Virginia then seems to have been to give the combatants names expressive of the plaintiff's theory of the merits of the controversy. So on June 1st, 1782 Timothy Goodtitle filed his declaration in the District Court of Dumfries against Francis Wronghead, alleging that Charles Alexander, gentleman, had leased certain land to said Timothy, from which he had been ejected by Wronghead. In due course Janet Birch and her husband intervened, confessing lease, entry and ouster, and agreeing to defend only on the ground of title. The land in suit lay just east of the villages shown on the modern maps as Pleasant Valley and Naucks. Luckily for the antiquarian, the proceedings were recorded in the first Land Suits book of the Dumfries District Court. When that court was abolished the book was turned over to the county court of Prince William. Two other suits were filed by Alexander at the same time which were held in abeyance to await the decision of the first suit. I cannot locate the land involved in them. The defendants may have derived their titles from the Robertsons, or from Carlyle or Ramsey. The record in the land suits book fills 230 pages, and consists mainly of the report of the surveyor, Robert Brooke, depositions and copies of patents, deeds and wills put in evidence as exhibits. The surveys made by Brooke were transmitted to the Court of Appeals at Richmond and were probably destroyed in the great fire of April, 1865. Besides the Howsing and Robertson patents, Brooke, at the request of the plaintiff or defendant surveyed or platted upwards of twenty other patents. If his plats had survived, we should have valuable map of the original patents along the Potomac from the Mathews patent south of Hunting Creek to the Robertson patent below Pimmitt run, as well as a number of inland patents. About thirty witnesses testified. Most of the depositions related to the location of notched corner trees, blazed line trees, old fords over Hunting Creek. Witnesses and chain carriers of surveys in the previous suits gave their recollections. Though not relevant, the accretion and reliction along the water front of Pipers Island and Alexander's Island were gone into, a subject now engaging the attention of the boundary commission investigating the claims of the United States and Arlington County to the Virginia water front. Occasional items of human interest appear, as when old John Sommers, ninety-two years old, told how in 1715 he moved from Dogue Neck to a spot near the present Christ Church, and in 1723 he moved into the "forest" (it was next to William Henry Terrett's patent and near Bailey's Cross Roads), and in 1773 moved further into the "forest" to his son's house; that in old times he used to be a good deal with the surveyors and attended many surveys in the neighborhood of Hunting Creek; that he remembered the oak tree, a corner of Brent's patent; that John Ball (father of Moses Ball) took a parcel of boys to that tree, and got some switches and whipped the boys to make them remember Brent's corner. Brent's corner was also Ball's corner, as his deed was from Robert Brent.

Moses Ball described the making of the survey in the former suit of Carlyle vs Alexander. Col. Carlyle with his attorney, Mr. Sebastian, Charles Alexander, the surveyor and the chain carriers met at the hickory bush on Hunting Creek, the supposed southwest corner of the Alexander tract, and Col. Carlyle took out a bundle of papers and said it was the General Court's order to begin at this hickory bush and lay off the Howsing patent from it; how the surveyor's line followed a line of marked trees till he came to the Todd and Thomas patent when they failed him and he angled to another line of trees. Moses Ball also told of Hunting Creek in his boyhood days; of a salt house and boat house on the north bank, at which last a brig was built; of the upper and lower ford, of swimming across the creek below the boat house.

It appears from the printed report of the case in First Washington's Virginia reports, that the jury found for Alexander on a special verdict. A special verdict is a statement of facts agreed upon by counsel for the plaintiff and defendant and submitted to the jury. This special verdict stated that the original John Alexander entered on his patent in 1669 and was seized and possessed as the law requires, and that his successors in title were likewise seized and possessed until James Robertson recovered from Robert Alexander and was put in possession as the result of the decision of the General Court in 1765. It is difficult to conjecture at this distance of time why Janet Birch's lawyers agreed to the damaging admission that the Alexanders entered and were possessed of the land in controversy which lay between the north 6 degrees west line and the north 15 degrees west line. It would seem that their contention should have been that the west line of the patent should be run so as to include 6000 acres and no more and that the last or home line of the patent should be shortened to 400 poles to beginning. The real question was the construction of the Howsing patent. It was based upon the transportation of 120 emigrants at 50 acres per person and should have been held down to 6000 acres unless the metes and bounds demanded the inclusion of more land. Nothing on the record indicates that the Alexanders had twenty years adverse possession of the contested area prior to 1765 when James Robertson was put in possession by the decree of the General Court.

When the case was argued in the Court of Appeals counsel for Birch was reduced, by his unlucky admissions, to the futile arguments that the Howsing patent was void because the Crown had granted the Northern Neck to the Proprietors before 1669; that only a life estate passed to Howsing, because there were no words of inheritance in the grant; that there was no seal on the original patent. The Court of Appeals held, as it was almost bound to hold, that the admitted fact of possession by the Alexanders from 1669 to 1730, when Robertson got his patent, made the title good by possession in Robert Alexander, the second; that the subsequent ejection of the Alexanders in 1765 by the decree of the General Court and the possession of Robertson thereafter had not lasted the necessary twenty years when in 1782 Charles Alexander brought the present ejectment; that Charles Alexander should recover the half interest for which he sued.

So the long controversy ended. To what extent the Carlyle and Ramsey titles were affected by the other two suits filed by Charles Alexander, I cannot say. One of Charles Alexander's heirs devised land south of Four Mile Run "between the Washington Turnpike and the west boundary line commonly called the north 17 degrees west line".[48] North of the Robertson land lay the plantation of Constantia Chapman. She and her heirs continued in undisturbed possession. Perhaps one fourth of her 430 acre tract lay within the north 15 degrees west line and 13 acres of it was within the north 6 degrees west line. This last is shown on a plat of the division of Col. Gerard Alexander's estate as "Chapman's Interference",[49] and a map of the Custis estate at Arlington Mansion shows that George Washington Parke Custis acquiesced in this interference. In 1833, her grandson, Nathaniel Chapman was in undisputed possession of the whole tract which he conveyed to John B. Chapman.[50]

---

[48] Will of Charles Alexander, Jr., Arlington Co. Wills Book 1–297.

[49] Fairfax County Survey Book 1787–1856 p 61.

[50] Arlington D. B., V 2.

North of Chapman there appear to have been no pro-
ietary grants along the North 6 degrees west line, and no
one to contest the Alexander claim to the land between that
line and the north 15 degrees west line. Apparently Robert
Alexander, son of Col. Gerard Alexander took possession to
the exclusion of other representatives of the family. He
died in 1793, devising his estate to his two sons Robert and
Walter S. Alexander. This Robert died leaving two children, Edward H. and Ashton Albert Alexander. They conveyed their half interest to Anthony R. Fraser in 1834, and
the land, 400 acres, was partitioned by the Circuit Court of
Alexandria County between Fraser and Walter S. Alexander's heirs in 1840.[51] As late as 1900 one of Walter S.
Alexander's sons, the late Columbus Alexander, still owned
one hundred acres west of Fort Myer, one of the last remaining parts of the Howsing patent held by a descendant
of the first John Alexander.

There is little more to add about the subsequent his-
tory of the Howsing patent. Charles Alexander (1737–
1806) was the oldest son of John Alexander. He married
Frances Brown, a sister of Dr. Gustavus Brown of Port
Tobacco. He was a lawyer and conducted Alexander vs
Birch in person. He resided in Alexandria for a few years
and then built and lived at "Preston" on a hill overlooking
Four Mile Run. He was a signer of the Fairfax County
Resolutions of 1774; a justice of the Fairfax County Court
and vestryman of Fairfax parish. He died intestate, leaving his widow, Frances and six children, Gustavus B., who
returned to the ancient family home of Caledon, where he
lived until his death in 1860; Charles Jr., William B., Richard B., Lee Massey and Susanna, the wife of George Chapman, Jr. He left a considerable personal estate and the
large tract south of Four Mile Run. This was divided
among his children, some of whom built homes on it. His
son Charles Jr. died in 1812 testate, leaving a widow Mary
Bowles, and children Charles Armstead, William F.,

[51] Arlington Co. Land Suits, A–52.

Marianna, Louisa E., Laura and Frances. Frances married Thomas Swann, a lawyer who practiced in Washington and Alexandria. They built Oakville on the south bank of Four Mile Run, but abandoned it after the railroad was opened close by. They then built a modest home, "Mount Auburn", on a tract nearer the river. It is owned and occupied by their granddaughter, Miss Helen Chapman Calvert, and is perhaps the sole fragment of the Howsing patent which has never been out of the Alexander family. [52]

Robert Alexander (son of Col. Gerard Alexander) died in 1793 shortly after taking Abingdon back. His will was proved in Fairfax and indicates that he left a large landed estate. [53] As stated he left a widow, Marianna T., who remarried one Greenfield, and the two sons named above, Robert and Walter S. Commissioners were appointed by the Fairfax court to divide the Abingdon tract up to the North 6 degrees west line between the sons. Robert Jr. however soon became involved and his portion of the estate was sold under order of court in 1807 to George Wise, who soon after acquired the interest of Walter S. Alexander. In 1837 Geo. Wise conveyed the portion of the Abingdon tract fronting on the river to Alexander Hunter whose wife Louisa Chapman Hunter owned the Summer Hill farm of the Chapmans adjoining on the south. Alexander Hunter was U. S. marshal for the District of Columbia and a descendant of the first John Alexander. He willed the Abingdon property to his brother Bushrod W. Hunter in trust for Alexander, son of Bushrod. Both Bushrod Hunter and his son entered the Confederate Army and the property was confiscated by the U. S. After the Civil War, it was restored to Alexander Hunter as the result of a suit. [54] In 1851 Louisa Hunter, widow of Alexander Hunter, conveyed away the Summer Hill farm, thus terminating the 125 years Chapman ownership.

---

[52] Days in an Old Town. Betty Carter Smoot.

[53] Fairfax Wills, F-219.

[54] Columbia Historical Society, Vol. 31, 32, article by Chas. O. Paullin.

The tract between Abingdon and Arlington was assigned to Philip Alexander in the division of Col. Gerard Alexander's estate. It included Holmes Island, which by this time began to be called Alexander Island. He died in 1790, leaving sons, Philip, George, Gerard, Austin and Charles. His will[55] devised to his eldest son Philip "the island and plantation whereon I now live as far as the road that goes from Alexandria to Georgetown". This Philip in 1808 deeded a part of this tract lying near the river, to his youngest brother Charles, and in 1811 conveyed the balance of his land to William Henry Washington.[56] Apparently he was much indebted at this time, as Washington shortly afterward conveyed the tract to William Brent in trust to sell to raise money to pay Alexander's debts.[57]

There stands on the northern part of this tract, close to the Alexandria and Georgetown road a fine old brick house, consisting of a central building, wings and a large outbuilding. The site was chosen with care and commands a noble prospect of the river and the hills beyond. The house was until recently the property of the Hon. Phil Campbell. It must have been built by one of the Philip Alexanders just named, probably toward the end of the eighteenth century. It is the most impressive memorial left of the Alexander tenure of the Howsing patent.

---

[55] Fairfax Wills, E–373.
[56] Arlington Co. D. B., V–30.
[57] Arlington Co. D. B., B. B.–102.

WASHINGTON FOREST

Four Mile Run is an affluent of the Potomac River eight or nine miles long draining the southwesterly part of Arlington County and a small portion of Fairfax County. In the earlier patents it was usually called Four Mile Creek or Four Miles Creek. The origin of the name is fairly obvious. It was the first considerable estuary on the Virginia side above Great Hunting Creek and was about four miles north of it.

If the Indians gave the run a name it has not survived. The name first appears on the Virginia land records in 1694 when the great tract afterward known as Ravensworth was granted to William Fitzhugh.[1] The northeast corner of this patent is recited to be a "marked red oak standing on the east side of a run of Four Mile Creek." This corner was far away from the Potomac River, somewhere in the vicinity of Falls Church. Assuredly neither Fitzhugh nor his surveyor coined the name. It already existed and must have been assigned prior to 1694.

The lower reaches of the run and the surrounding territory passed definitively from the Crown to private ownership by patent of Sir William Berkeley to Robert Howsing, dated October 19, 1669. Howsing was a Welch ship captain trading in Virginia, and shortly after assigned his patent to John Alexander.

The greater portion of the Howsing patent remained in the Alexander family for more than a century. There were no further patents for the inland land along Four Mile Run until the beginning of the eighteenth century. The Indian war that led to Bacon's Rebellion had its origin in the Potomac region and the northward advance of

---

[1] Northern Neck Land Grants (hereafter called N.N.), No. 2, p. 14.

settlement was delayed. The only part of Fairfax County actually settled in the seventeenth century was the southern part along the Occoquan, Pohick, Accotink and Hunting Creeks. The historial markers on the road from Washington to Fredericksburg give the correct dates of the earliest patents, but many of them were abandoned and escheated, and were re-granted later to the actual settlers.

The Howsing patent was a grant from the Crown. All subsequent grants along Four Mile Run were made by the proprietors of the Northern neck. The explanation is that in the interval, the title to all the unseated land between the Potomac and Rappahannock Rivers, called the Northern Neck, had passed by a series of charters from the Crown to certain proprietary overlords whose title finally became vested in Lord Culpeper. He died in 1689, leaving an only daughter who succeeded to the proprietorship, and married Thomas, fifth Lord Fairfax. [2]

Neither she nor her husband ever came to Virginia. They were represented by agents, who made grants in their names and collected the quit-rents for them. By 1690 the vigorous objections to the charters, raised by the colonial legislature and governors, had been overruled by the law officers of the Crown and the resident agent of the proprietors opened a land office in the colony and began issuing grants. The Fitzhugh grant of Ravensworth was one of the earliest.

Two of the best known agents for the proprietors were Thomas Lee, the builder of Stratford, and the ancestor of a long line of illustrious soldiers and statesmen, and Robert Carter, commonly known as "King Carter" from his great estate and dominating personality.

It was during Robert Carter's second agency that patents were issued for most of the land bordering on Four Mile Run, lying back of the Alexander tract, including the two tracts subsequently acquired by George Washington which form the subject of this paper.

---

[2] Fauquier during the Proprietorship. H. C. Groome.

On the death of Lady Catherine Fairfax, the proprietorship of the Northern Neck passed by her will to her son Thomas, sixth Lord Fairfax in tail male. He first visited Virginia in 1735, remaining two years and then going back to England. In 1747 he returned to Virginia to live out there his long life of 88 years. For several years he made his home with William Fairfax, his cousin and land agent, at Belvoir (now Camp Humphries) where William Fairfax had built a noble mansion on a steep bluff overlooking the Potomac. It was there he commissioned the young Washington to make surveys for him beyond the Blue Ridge and in Culpeper County.

About 1751 Lord Fairfax established himself at Greenway Court in the Shenandoah Valley, and there he lived until his death in 1781.

The grants of lands in the Northern Neck were recorded in large folio volumes, now stored in the Capitol building in Richmond. Considering the many removals they have undergone, it is remarkable that the series has survived in its entirety. Only a few pages are missing and a few mutilated and torn. Begun in 1690, the manuscript volumes grew to 25 before Lord Fairfax's death. Each successive agent took over the volumes containing the grants of his predecessors, and added his own grants made in the name of the proprietor, but signed by himself. After he established himself in Virginia, Lord Fairfax carried the land grant books with him over the Blue Ridge to Greenway Court where he built a small stone office for their accommodation. Greenway Court is gone but the little office building is still standing.

In 1785 the Legislature of Virginia passed "An Act for the Safe Keeping of the Land Papers of the Northern Neck," directing the removal of the land grant books to Richmond. Thereupon followed the final migration of these valuable records. They are the source books of title to some or all of the land in 19 counties of Virginia and 5 of West Virginia.

41

The earliest grant of land bordering on Four Mile Run by the proprietors of the Northern Neck, was made January 21, 1705, "in ye fourth year of the reign of our Sovereign Lady Anne" by Margueritte, Lady Culpeper, Thomas, Lord Fairfax, and Catherine, his wife, proprietors of the Northern Neck of Virginia, by Robert Carter their agent, to William Struttfield of the County of Westmoreland. It conveyed 535 acres in the County of Stafford on the south side of Four Mile Creek, adjoining the Alexander land on the west, running up the stream about a mile and extending south to the neighborhood of the Episcopal High School, and reserved an annual rent of one shilling sterling money for every 50 acres so granted. [3]

Other grants followed quickly. In 1707 Thomas Pearson was given 660 acres in Stafford County on "Four Mile Creek, main run, on the lower side thereof." [4] This land extended along the south side of the run, about three-quarters of a mile. It appears to have been located opposite the present Bluemont Junction, and extended south to include Munson Hill. Before 1730 Four Mile Run was in Stafford County. From 1730 to 1742 it was in Prince William County, and after the latter year it was in Fairfax County.

In 1713, a tract of 795 acres between the branches of Four Mile Run and the head of Spout Run was granted to Rev. James Brechin. [5] This land appears to have included much of the present village of Ballston.

In 1719 John Todd and Evan Thomas patented 1215 acres on the north side of Four Mile Run, [6] adjoining the Alexander lands on the west, extending up the run about 2 miles to the branch known as Doctor's Run, and including

---

[3] N.N. 3 p. 121.

[4] N.N. 3 p. 225.

[5] N.N. 5 p. 44. Rev. James Brechin was the minister of Cople Parish, Westmoreland County, Va. Magazine of History & Biography, Vol. 2, p. 14.

[6] N.N. 5, p. 212.

the present colored settlement of Nauck and Green Valley.

In 1724 and 1729, Capt. Simon Pearson, son of Thomas Pearson, patented two tracts south of Four Mile Run, but not immediately bordering on it, containing 1279 and 331 acres respectively.[7] The first was in the neighborhood of Falls Church, and the second included the present Bailey's Cross Roads.

In 1730 Simon Pearson and James Going patented 650 acres on the north side of Four Mile Run.[8] This included the land where Wilson Boulevard now crosses the run.

In 1731 Simon Pearson and Gabriel Adams patented 708 acres[9] further west on the same side of the run, and extending back to the long branch of Pimmitt Run. This tract is crossed by the road connecting East Falls Church with Washington.

In 1725 Robert Bates of Stafford County got a grant for 525 acres on the north side of Four Mile Run west of Todd and Thomas and east of the tract subsequently patented by John Colville. The Lee Boulevard passes through it.[10]

In 1729 William Gunnell of Westmoreland County got two patents for 400 and 250 acres bordering on the run, the first north of Falls Church and the second on the south side of the run, adjoining Thomas Pearson's patent on the west.[11] He has descendants in Fairfax County.

In 1731 Maj. John Colville took out a grant for 1246 acres on the north side of Four Mile Run which included Lubber Run, the present subdivision of Bon Air Veitch, and extended to or beyond Hall's Hill.[12]

---

[7] N.N. A 57 & C 27.
[8] N.N. C, p. 118.
[9] N.N. D, p. 40.
[10] N.N., A-p. 146.
[11] N.N., C-; 8 and 9.
[12] N.N., E, p. 131.

In 1742 and 1748 John and Moses Ball got the patents on the south side of Four Mile Run.[13] It is believed this enumeration comprises all the land grants on the run except the two that Washington bought.

These patents show that the settlement of the Four Mile Run valley began shortly after 1700. By 1733 a sufficient population had settled in the neighborhood to justify the erection of a wooden church on the site of the present Falls Church, where there was already a cross roads.

The land later acquired by Washington was made up of two patents issued to Stephen Gray and Gabriel Adams respectively. Gray's patent dated in July, 1724,[14] was for 378 acres in the County of Stafford, "Lying on the lower side of the main run of Four Mile Creek, beginning at a white oak standing on said main run, south side, about a half a mile above a mill called Chubb's Mill, in or near a a line of Major Robert Alexander's and opposite the land granted to Mr. Evan Thomas and Mr. John Todd." As it turned out, Gray's patent attempted to appropriate considerable land embraced in the prior patent to Struttfield, and its effective point of beginning was about a mile west of Chubb's Mill and the Alexander line. Its western boundary was the land later granted to Moses Ball.

Gabriel Adams' patent was dated September 19, 1730,[15] and called for 790 acres. It adjoined Gray's patent on the south and Capt. Simon Pearson's patent on the west. Its eastern boundary line was the small stream called Lucky Run, a branch of Four Mile Run, and it extended south across the present Alexandria and Leesburg Road and the Seminary Road.

Nothing is known of Stephen Gray except that he resided in Stafford County which then embraced the whole river front north of Westmoreland County. Gabriel Adams was a man of some local consequence. He had

---

[13] These patents are the subject of the last of these papers.

[14] N.N. A, p. 44.

[15] N.N. C, p. 136.

other grants on Four Mile and Holmes Runs and must have resided somewhere in the present Fairfax County, as he was a member of the original vestry of Truro Parish (which included Pohick Church), organized in 1732.

He died in 1761 in Loudoun County where his will is recorded (Wills A–35). He had a brother, William Adams, who operated a mill where the Columbia turnpike crosses Holmes Run. It, or a later one on the same site, still exists, though abandoned.

In 1733, by deed of lease and release, Gabriel Adams conveyed his tract to John Mercer of Stafford County.[16] At the same time, Mercer caused Gray's original patent to be recorded in the Prince William County Court which entered on its record a notation that "the deed was presented into Court by John Mercer and on his motion admitted to record."[17] The land was then in Prince William County and Mercer evidently regarded the record of the patent on his motion as passing Gray's title to him.

John Mercer, of Marlborough (1704-1768), was an emigrant from Ireland. He was a planter, a lawyer, and the author of a compilation of the laws of Virginia, known as Mercer's Abridgement. His plantation was on the Potomac at the end of the peninsula formed by Aquia and Potomac Creeks. The place still bears the name of Marlborough Point. It had been designated as a town and laid off into lots as far back as 1691 by an act of the Virginia Assembly. The era of towns on the Potomac was then still in the far future. Mercer eventually bought up the whole of the abortive town, with adjoining tracts, and made a plantation of them. He was probably the first lawyer Washington consulted. The evidence is an entry in Washington's cash book and ledger:

"1755, Jany 11th. Cash by Mr. Mer-   £   s   d
        cer for his opinion of the devise
        of my brother's negroes,   1   1   6

---

[16] Prince William D. B.–B.44.
[17] Prince William D. B.–B.49.

By ditto for his opinion on the   £   s   d
devise of Mount Vernon tract
to me,   1   1   6[18]

This entry shows that as early as 1755 Washington was taking advice upon the clause of his brother Lawrence's will, which provided that if George died without issue, the Mount Vernon tract should go to Lawrence's older brother Augustine; but that complication, and the story of its unravelment, is no part of the history of the Four Mile Run tract.

John Mercer's name appears frequently in the Northern Neck land grants. Among other tracts he patented 1000 acres in the present Fairfax County between the north and south runs of Pohick Creek. This latter tract he conveyed to his sons George and James Mercer, [19] by a deed recorded in the General Court of the Colony at Williamsburg in 1759. The records of that court were burned long ago, but the fact that such a deed was made and recorded is recited in another deed recorded in Fairfax County in 1774, by James Mercer, conveying his moiety of the Pohick Run tract. [20] As George and James Mercer were then offering John Mercer's Four Mile Run land for sale, and as there is no existing record of a conveyance from John Mercer to them, it becomes almost certain that the deed recorded in the General Court also included that tract.

George and James Mercer, who acquired title to the Four Mile Run tract by the lost deed from their father, were men of some note in the later colonial period of Virginia.

George Mercer, the elder son, was intimately associated with Washington in the French and Indian War. He was a lieutenant in the campaign that ended at Great Meadows; a captain in Braddock's expedition. When, the

---

[18] Ledgers A–60.
[19] N.N. B., p. 55.
[20] Fairfax D. B.–L. 269.

next year, Washington was made a colonel and entrusted with the defense of the frontier against the destructive Indian raids, he made George Mercer his aide-de-camp and as such, he attended Washington on his journey to Boston to confer with Governor Shirley. In 1761 he was Washington's colleague in the House of Burgesses, both representing Frederick County. Mercer then went to London as the agent of the Ohio Company. While there he penned a description of his former commander's personal appearance. It has been often quoted, but will bear quoting again:

"Although distrusting my ability to give an adequate account of the personal appearance of Col. George Washington, late Commander of the Virginia Provincial troops, I shall, as you request, attempt the portraiture. He may be described as being as straight as an Indian, measuring six feet two inches in his stockings, and weighing 175 pounds when he took his seat in the House of Burgesses in 1759. His frame is padded with well-developed muscles, indicating great strength. His bones and joints are large, as are his feet and hands.

"He is wide shouldered, but has not a deep or round chest; is neat waisted, but is broad across the hips, and has rather long legs and arms. His head is well shaped though not large, but is gracefully poised on a superb neck. A large and straight rather than prominent nose; blue-gray penetrating eyes, which are widely separated and overhung by a heavy brow. His face is long rather than broad, with high round cheek bones, and terminates in a good firm chin. He has a clear though rather a colorless pale skin, which burns with the sun. A pleasing, benevolent, though a commanding countenance, dark brown hair, which he wears in a cue.

"His mouth is large and generally firmly closed, but which from time to time discloses some defective teeth. His features are regular and placid, with all the muscles of his face under perfect control, though flexible and expressive of deep feeling when moved by emotions. In conversation he looks you full in the face, is deliberate, deferential and engaging. His voice is agreeable rather than strong. His demeanor at all times composed and dignified. His movements and gestures are graceful, his walk majestic, and he is a splendid horseman."[21]

When the Stamp Act was passed Mercer was appointed "Chief distributor of stamps" for Virginia. He returned to the Colony but the storm that the Act raised forced his resignation, and although he had not been more than ten days in America, he found himself "under a necessity of immediately returning to England," where he remained the rest of his life.[22]

Naturally, his ancestral estate at Marlborough suffered from his absence. Washington assisted him in disposing of his bounty land in western Virginia, and so became acquainted with his affairs. Writing in 1775, Washington said:

"That Colo. Mercer has been a considerable loser in the management of his Estate here, nobody will deny; but has not every gentleman in this country whose other avocations, or whose inclinations would not permit them to devote a large portion of their time & Attention to the management of their own Estates, shared the same fate? Our Gazettes afford but too many melancholy proofs of it in the sales which are daily advertised; the nature of a Virginia Estate being such that without close application it never fails bringing the proprietors in Debt annually, as Negroes must be clothed & fed, taxes paid, etc., etc., whether anything is made or not."[23]

George Mercer died in England in 1784 in embarrassed circumstances.

James Mercer, the younger brother and resident owner, was the second son of John Mercer of Marlborough. He graduated from William and Mary College in 1767; be-

---

[21] J. M. Toner, George Washington as an Inventor, etc.

[22] History of Virginia. Charles Campbell.

[23] Writings of Washington (Ford), Vol. II, p. 469.

came a lawyer; was a member of the House of Burgesses, the Virginia Conventions; the Committee of Safety; a delegate to the Continental Congress, and a Judge of the First Court of Appeals of Virginia.[24] In 1774 he was living in Fredericksburg, and Washington's Diaries mention dining with him several times. He died in 1793.

George Mason called Washington's attention to the Mercer tract on Four Mile Run as a desirable purchase. In a letter from Gunston Hall, dated December 21, 1773, he wrote:

"I have by me Mr. Mercer's title deeds for his lands on Pohick Run and on Four Mile Run in this county, wh. I have hitherto endeavored to sell for him in vain, for as he left the price entirely to me, I could not take less for them than if they had been my own; this difficulty will not be lessened, but the contrary by your becoming the purchaser. ... Had I sold them to an indifferent purchaser, I should in the common way of business have stretched my demand so far as it would bear, but between you and Mr. Mercer, would fain consider myself as a mutual Friend and arbiter, and from my connections with him, I know he would wish me to act in that manner, which renders it an affair of some delicacy, and takes it out of the common mode of business. ... The tract upon Four Mile Run is contained in two patents, one granted to Stephen Gray for 378 acres, and the other to Gabriel Adams for 790 acres. They appear by the plat to over-measure considerably, and contain, clear of Struttfield's elder patent (with which they interfere) 1225 acres. I have formerly been upon this land, but its so many years ago that I know very little of it from my own knowledge, but from the best information I have had, that part of it upon Four Mile Run (in Stephen Gray's patent) is tollerable good, and the other mean; but from its vicinity to Alexandria, which now bids fair to be a very considerable town, I think it must be worth £1000 curr'y. ... Upon the whole, sir, if you will appoint any day after

[24] Lanman's Biographical Annals.

Christmas, I will wait [upon] you & we will ride over the land together, when we shall both be better able to judge of its value."

"There was some little difficulty in the title from Stephen Gray wh. Mr. Mercer has been very candid in laying open to me and wh. Mr. Pendleton (whose opinion I have) has cleared up in a very satisfactory manner."[25]

The difficulty in Gray's title must have been the want of a deed from him to John Mercer, and Mr. Pendleton's opinion, we may conjecture, was to the effect that as John Mercer had possession of the original patent and moved its admission to record in the Prince William County Court, that was sufficient evidence of the assignment of the patent to him.

If Washington and Mason rode over the land together, the Diaries do not report it, but Washington decided to buy, and on December 26, 1774, wrote to James Mercer from Mount Vernon:

"I cannot say but that I should have liked to have had 1224 acres of land warranted to me, instead of your granting 1200 acres more or less; for as it was upon the presumption that the tracts of Gray and Adams contained this quantity, clear of disputed bounds, that I agreed to give the price I did; so if it falls short (I mean more than is generally allowed for variation of instruments) I shall not much like, nor indeed think myself bound by it; and am inclined to think (as Mr. Carlyle also does) that Hough must have made some mistake in his measurement, as the original patents to Adams and Gray together contain no more than 1168 acres, whilst it appears that Adams' patent runs into Gray's, and one half, or near it, of Gray's is taken away by Strutfield's. Notwithstanding all which, Hough, you say (for I have no plat or report of his) makes 56 acres more than is granted by both patents; at the same time he differs but little (as I perceive by your plat) from the original courses and distances. . . ."

[25] Letters to Washington. S. M. Hamilton, Vol. IV, p. 286.

"It was my intention to have run round the lines of these tracts and tried the contents of them myself; but I have never been a day well since my return from Frederick, nor a day without company. If you have Adams' conveyance, I should be glad to be furnished with it when you send the copy of the power of attorney, to McCoul and Blair, as I have no paper relative to this land, except an unattested copy of the Proprietor's deed to him.

"I have wrote to your Brother since I came home. I intended a short letter, just to advise him of the amount of the sales, but insensibly run into a long one . . . ."[26]

This tract of some 1200 acres was then all woodland, and near half of it is woodland today. Its northern boundary followed the windings of Four Mile Run for about a mile and a half from a point about half a mile west of the mill standing at the crossing of the Columbia Turnpike at Barcroft, down the run to the mouth of Lucky Run, about a mile east of Barcroft. It stretched southward across the Alexandria and Leesburg Road, and on across the road connecting Bailey's Cross Roads with the Virginia Theologcal Seminary known as Seminary Road.

In 1775 there was but one public road through the tract. This was the "old" Alexandria and Leesburg Road. The course of this "old road through the tract was nearly that now followed by the Seminary Road. On the eastern boundary of the tract this road forked, one branch leading to Alexandria, the other to Cameron, the name given to the ford over Hunting Creek where the main road from Alexandria to Fredericksburg crossed. The modern "Telegraph Road" crosses Hunting Creek at the same place.

The purchase price was 892 pounds or about $7.00 an acre, but owing to certain difficulties in the transmission of title of George Mercer's half interest, Washington paid James Mercer his half of the money and gave a bond for the payment of George Mercer's half interest. The Mercers

---

[26] Writings of Washington (Ford), 2-446.

made a handsome profit on the transaction which is more than can be said for their illustrious vendee. When Custis Lee sold the tract in parcels a century later, he got about $10.00 per acre for the better portions, and gave away the rest to the Trustees of the Theological Seminary of Virginia.

The deed from James Mercer and the attorneys and agents of George Mercer to Washington, was dated December 12, 1774, and proved and admitted to record on October 15, 1775, in the General Court at the Capitol in Williamsburg. The records of that court were destroyed by fire in 1865 but the facts are recited in a later deed recorded at Fairfax Court House. In October, 1775, Washington was no longer in Virginia. In the preceding June he had set out from Philadelphia to take command of the Continental Army at Cambridge, and the running of the lines of the tracts and the trying their contents was deferred until he returned to private life eight years later.

In 1785 he again took up the matter of surveying the tract and his diaries contain the following:

"Thursday April 21, 1785. After an early dinner I went up in my barge to Abingdon . . . Took my instruments with intent to survey the land I hold by purchase on 4 Mile Run of George and James Mercer, Esqrs.

"Friday, 22d. Took an early breakfast at Abingdon and accompanied by Doctor Stewart and Lund Washington, and having sent for Mr. Moses Ball (who attended) I went to a corner of the above land within about three poles of the run [4 Miles Run], a white oak, 18 inches in diameter on the side of a hill, abt. 150 yards below the ruins of an old mill and 100 below a small Branch which comes in on the No.Et. side, and after having run one course and part of another, my servant William [one of the Chain Carriers] fell and broke the pan of his knee, wch. put a stop to my surveying, and with difficulty I was able to get him to Abingdon, being obliged to get a sled to carry him on, as he could neither walk, stand or ride." [27]

---

[27] Diaries, Vol. 2, page 366.

William Lee, the chain bearer, was Washington's favorite body-servant "Billy." Savage's well known painting of the Washington "family group" shows him standing in the background.

Paul Leicester Ford's admirable "True George Washington" gives such a pleasant account of Washington's affection for this trusted slave that I quote it: "From this injury Lee never quite recovered yet he started to accompany his master to New York in 1789, only to give out on the road. He was left at Philadelphia, and Lear wrote to Washington's agent that 'The President will thank you to propose it to Will to return to Mt. Vernon when he can be removed, for he cannot be of any service here, and perhaps will require a person to attend upon him constantly. If he should incline to return to Mt. Vernon, you will be so kind as to have him sent in the first vessel that sails for Alexandria, after he can be moved with safety–but if he is still anxious to come on here, the President would gratify him altho' he will be troublesome. He has been an old and faithful servant, this is enough for the President to gratify him in every reasonable wish'." [28]

Washington's will gave Lee his freedom, food, clothing and a yearly allowance of $30; "and this I give him as a testimony of my sense of his attachment to me and for his faithful services during the Revolutionary War."

The spot where Washington began his survey is still easily identifiable. The "small branch which comes in on the No.Et. side" now makes its way to Four Mile Run under a railroad culvert, and the depression of the old mill race can still be traced. Washington sent for Moses Ball because he had patented and was then living on a small tract of 91 acres, adjoining Stephen Gray's patent on the west.

The old mill whose ruins Washington mentioned must have stood on Moses Ball's land, and presumably was built by him or his neighbor, John Ball. As the patent of the

[28] Ford. "True George Washington," page 151.

latter dated from 1742, and that of the former from 1748, the mill must have had a brief life.

Washington's first attempt to survey his Four Mile Run lands was thwarted by the accident to his servant. It was not until the next year that he finished his survey. His diary of May 5, 1786, contains this entry:

"Set out early from Abingdon, and beginning at the upper corner of my land (on 4 Miles run) a little below an old mill; I ran the tract agreeable to the courses and distances of a plat made thereof by John Hough in the year 1766 (Novr.) in the presence of Colo. Carlyle and Mr. James Mercer. Not having Hough's field notes, and no corner trees being noted in this Plat, I did not attempt to look for lines; but allowing one degree for the variation of the Compass since the survey above mentioned was made, I run the courses and distances only, and was unable for want of time, to do more than run the lines that brought me to the run again; the Meanders of wch. must be run at some other time, in order to ascertain with precision the quantity of Land which is contained. Upon the whole I found this tract fully equal to my expectations. The whole of it is well wooded, some part is pretty well timbered, and generally speaking, it is level. About the main road at the South of the tract, trespasses (on the wood) had been made but in a degree less than I expected to find; and as I run the lines set down, with the variation, I run into the field lately Colo. Carlyle's (now Whiting's) so as to cut off 12 or 15 acres of his enclosure, and made the plat close very well to the run.

"Returned at night to Abingdon being attended in the labors of the day by Doctr. Stuart." [29]

---

[29] Diaries, No. 3, p. 55. "In the presence of Colonel Carlyle" does not mean that he was present with Washington in 1786, for he died in 1780, but signifies that he was a witness to Hough's survey in 1766. Colonel Carlyle was the builder of the well known Carlyle house in Alexandria, and had acquired Struttfield's patent, which adjoined Washington's land on the east.

The devolution of the patent from Struttfield to Carlyle Fairfax Whiting is shown by exhibits filed in the suit of Alexander vs Birch.

Deed dated March 8, 1710 from Struttfield to John Bushrod both of Cople parish, Westmoreland County.

Deed dated Jan. 20, 1719 from John Bushrod (1663–1719) to Nicholas Merewether, son of William Merewether and Elizabeth his wife, daughter of said Bushrod.

From Nicholas Merewether (1699–1739) the title passed by descent to his daughter Mildred, the wife of Col. John Sym of Hanover County.

In 1756 John Sym (1729–after 1776) bound himself by bond to John Carlyle, that when his wife Mildred became 21 years of age, she would join in a deed conveying the property. Mildred died under twenty-one leaving an only son and heir John.

On July 20th, 1784 John Sym (1752–1793) and Sully his wife conveyed to Carlyle Fairfax Whiting.

John Carlyle (1720–1780) came to Virginia from Scotland about 1740. He was twice married, first, to Sarah, daughter of William Fairfax of Belvoir. By her he had two daughters, Sarah who married William Herbert, and Ann Fairfax who married Henry Whiting of Berkeley county. Carlyle's second marriage was with Sybil West by whom he had a son. George William, an officer in the Continental Army killed in the battle of Eutaw Springs. John Carlyle was buried in the Presbyterian church yard in Alexandria. His will, dated April 5, 1780 devised the residue of his extensive estate, to his son George William Carlyle, but in case of his death under twenty-one and without issue, then to his grandsons, John Carlyle Herbert and Carlyle Fairfax Whiting. The son left no issue. A division of the division of the residue of the estate between the two grandsons was made by the county court of Fairfax. The Struttfield patent was assigned to Carlyle Fairfax Whiting.

He made his home on the land and gave it the name of Morven. He probably built the large frame house near the Alexandria and Leesburg road. On his death in 1834 the estate consisted of 640 acres. His will did not change the course of descent. He left a widow, Sarah, and five children, Charles H., George W. C., Fairfax H., William W. and Ellen M. The estate was partitioned in the chancery court of Alexandria County. Charles H. Whiting was allotted the mansion

Abingdon, as is well known, was the home on the Potomac, north of Four Mile Run, that John Parke Custis had purchased of Robert Alexander. After standing for a century and three-quarters it was burned about two years ago. After Custis' death his widow, Eleanor Calvert Custis, married Dr. David Stuart, who attended Washington on this survey. They were then living at Abingdon. Dr. Stuart owned an estate in Fairfax called Hope Park, and later purchased another estate in the county, about a mile south of Annandale on which he built a noble house that he named Ossian to which he and his family moved after vacating Abingdon. It is still standing and is one of the show places of the county. Washington thought highly of Dr. Stuart and appointed him one of the Commissioners of the Federal City. They corresponded throughout Washington's presidency, Washington desiring the doctor to keep him informed of public opinion in Maryland and Virginia, "not so much of what may be thought commendable parts, if any, of my conduct, as of those which may be conceived to be of a different complexion." [30]

Some of the current criticism that Stuart transmitted in compliance with this request irritated Washington, for he replied. "For I can truly say, I had rather be at Mount Vernon with a friend or two about me, than to be attended at the seat of government by the officers and representatives of every power in Europe." [31] Though written in vexation, the statement was but the sober truth. Such was his love for Mount Vernon and his zest in farming it, that he never seemed wholly happy when away from it. "Agriculture has ever been the most favorite amusement of my life" he once wrote.

---

house and two hundred acres. Fairfax H. and Ellen M. received other portions. About 1870 the bulk of the Morven estate was acquired by Courtney Smith, whose heirs continued to own it until recently.

[30] Writings, Vol. II, p. 405.
[31] Writings, Vol. II, p. 482.

The final steps vesting in Washington a satisfactory title to this tract are set out in a deed of May 22, 1787, recorded in Fairfax County, between James Mercer of Spottsylvania County of the one part, and his Excellency George Washington of Fairfax County, of the other part,[32] which recites:

"that George and James Mercer were on February 23d, 1772, seised as tenants in common of certain land in Fairfax County, and George Mercer residing then in London did by deed of lease . . . put the same in mortgage to John H. Casenave . . . and Elias Lindo of London, exchange brokers, by the description of all his farm lands in the County of Fairfax, in the Province of Virginia, and these three gave a letter of attorney to Neil McCoul and Alexander Blair of Fredericksburg dated February 13th, 1772 empowering them to sell said lands, and said McCoul and Blair sold the same to George Washington, and said James Mercer also joined to convey his half interest . . . and it is considered that the execution thereof was defective; and said George Mercer afterward became greatly indebted, and said attorneys never proceeded further saying that they took a bond from said George Washington for £450 for George Mercer's share, and George Mercer never returned to America, and died in 1784, leaving James Mercer his sole heir, and said George Washington is willing to complete his purchase by paying the £450 for which he gave bond . . ."

While living in Philadelphia as President, Washington was much annoyed by wood cutting and other trespasses on his land. In a letter to Dr. Stuart who had written him about the matter, he said "Mr. Bushr. Washington a year or two ago was desired to commence a suit or suits against some of the trespassers, but whether he did or not, or what the result was I do not recollect ever to have heard."[33]

---

[32] Fairfax, D. B., Q–1, p. 406.

[33] Letters and Recollections of Geo. Washington, Tobias Lear. p. 165.

He also wrote to his manager at Mount Vernon, William Pearce, that he wanted the bounds of the Four Mile Run tract resurveyed and the corners marked "that the pretence of not knowing the lines may no longer be an excuse for the trespasses which are committed thereon;" that "Moses Ball if living must have some knowledge of the lines; Mr. Terret also, but as he is interested in this business and is accused of being a pretty considerable trespasser on the part which joins him, it would not be strange if corner and line trees are both cut down."[34]

About eight months before his death Washington again surveyed this tract and set down in his diary:

"April 3d, 1799. Went up to Four Mile Run to Run around my land there. Got on the grd. about 10 o'clock, and in Company with Captn. Terrett and Mr. Luke commenced the survey on Four Mile Run, and ran agreeably to the Notes taken. In the evening went to Alexa. and lodged myself at Mr. Fitzhugh's.

"Apr. 4th. Recommenced to survey at the upper end where we left off in Company with Colo. Little, Captn. Terrett and Mr. Wm. Adams and continued it agreeably to the notes until we came to 4 Mile Run again, which employed us until dark."[35]

The exterior lines of the tract were about eight miles long, and ran through heavily wooded country, and along the banks of a run with few or no paths. Surveying it was strenuous work for a man sixty-seven years old, even though the work was divided between two days, and the first day, according to the diary was "extreme cold, but I forgot to see what the mercury was."

Captain Terrett, Mr. Luke and Mr. William Adams were adjoining proprietors, and were present because the dividing lines between them and Washington were to be marked. Captain Terrett was William Henry Terrett, the same, whom Washington suspected of having com-

---

[34] Writings (Ford). Vol. 13, p. 157.
[35] Diaries, No. 4, p. 301.

58

mitted trespasses on his wood. He is represented by many descendants in Washington and Virginia, some living now in the vicinity of this tract. Mr. John Luke was the owner of land embracing the present Baileys Cross Roads.

Even the last survey did not satisfy Washington, for he wrote a few days later to Ludwell Lee, who lived at Shooter's Hill, where the Alexandria Reservoir is now located: "Having good information that some land which I hold on Four Mile Run was much deprecated on, I went up some short while ago to go around the lines and found the fact to be as reported, but not being able to ascertain all the corners, and those holding the adjacent lands not being present, I forebore to remark the lay of the lines, but since desirous of doing this and meeting with all the parties at the election—Monday next is fixed therefor; who have engaged to meet me at the beginning corner of Adams Patent (under which I hold) by nine o'clock that morning, where and when, being informed that you have land adjoining (mine), I should be glad to meet you. As you may not know where this corner is, I shall pass a little house at the junction of the Leesburg Road (a widow's) half an hour before nine on my way."[36]

Ludwell Lee had recently bought the land referred to from William Henry Terrett as shown by deed recorded X–226, land records of Fairfax County.

The Diaries of April 29 and 30, 1799, contain entries:

"Apr. 29. Went up to run around my land on 4 Mile Run. Lodged at Colo. Littles.

"Apr. 30th. Engaged in the same business as yesterday. Returned home in the afternoon."[37]

The "Colo. Little" mentioned was Colonel Charles Little whose home "Cleesh" stood on a hill overlooking Cameron Run and was on the direct road from Mount Vernon to the Four Mile Run tract. He owned a "quarter

---

[36] Washington Manuscripts L.C., Book 11, p. 82. The "widow" appears to have been the "widow Tucker" as the Fairfax Order Book (Sept. Term 1789) locates her land on the road to Falls Church in this neighborhood.

[37] Diaries, No. 4, p. 303.

on the road from "the widow Tuckers to Falls Church"[38] near the tract. He was a personal friend of Washington's later years. In his Recollections of Washington, George Washington Parke Custis reproduced a facsimile of Washington's last survey of the tract showing its outlines.[39] A photograph of the survey accompanies this article. It is not certain whether the survey was made from the field notes of the survey of May 5, 1786, or of April 3–4, 1799. Washington intended to build a mill on his Four Mile Run land, but never did so.

When Washington bought this tract in 1775, the tax upon it was the annual quit rent payable to Lord Fairfax, of 2 shillings 6 pence per hundred acres, or a pound six shillings on the whole, about $6.50 a year. Allowing for the greater purchasing price of a dollar in the eighteenth century, this was still only a nominal tax on 1200 acres. The quit rents continued to be paid until Lord Fairfax's death in 1781.

A word about Lord Fairfax's last years may not be amiss here. The Commonwealth of Virginia dealt very gently with him. It is a record that every Virginian may be proud of. As he was a citizen of Virginia, the Act of 1777 forfeiting the property of British subjects did not apply to him. Feudal land tenures were abolished by that Act and the quit rents theretofore collected in the name of the King were done away with, but the Northern Neck was specifically excepted from the operation of the Act, and Lord Fairfax was suffered to continue in undisturbed possession of his proprietorship during the remainder of his life.[40] Arch-deacon Burnaby in his *Travels through North*

---

[38] Order Book Fairfax Co. 1789. Charles Little was the son of Andrew Little of Anandale, Scotland, and came to Virginia in 1768 with his two brothers. He was a cousin of Col. John Carlyle of Alexandria. Little purchased "Cleesh" from the executors of Col. John Colville. He was a pall bearer at Washington's funeral and died in 1813 at Denbeigh, Fairfax County (Powell–History of Alexandria).

[39] Recollections. G. W. P. Custis, p. 442.

[40] Fauquier during the Proprietorship. H. C. Groome. p. 219.

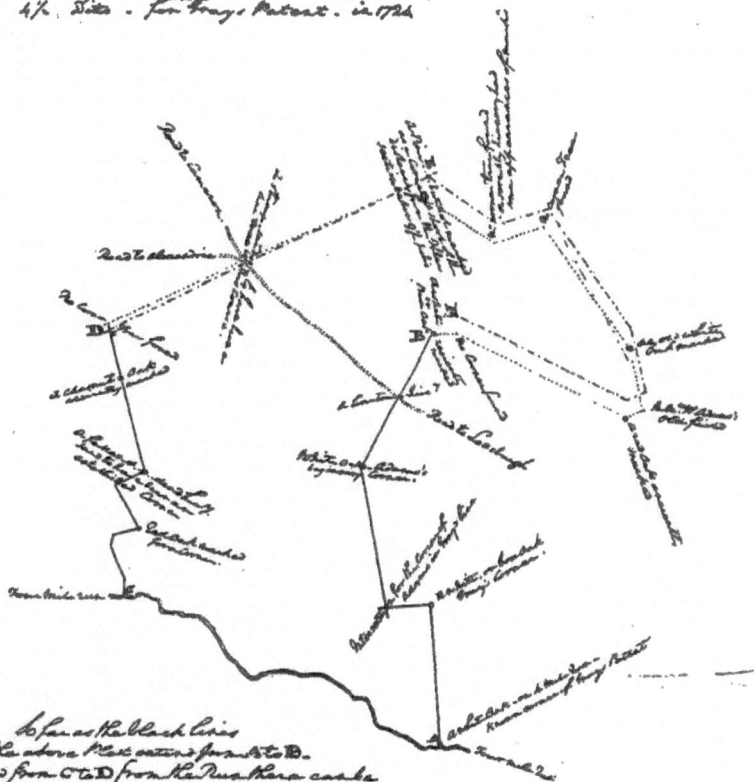

WASHINGTON'S SURVEY OF HIS FOUR MILE RUN LAND

America, referring to Lord Fairfax's life during the Revolution, says: "So unexceptional and disinterested was his behavior both public and private, and so generally was he beloved and respected, that during the late contest between Great Britain and America, he never met with the least insult or molestation from either party, but was suffered to go in his improvement and cultivation of the Northern Neck, a pursuit equally calculated for the comfort and happiness of individuals, for the general good of mankind." [41]

On his death, his proprietorship, five-sixths of which was entailed, passed by law to the next tenant in tail, a British subject and was confiscated by the State.

In his will Washington devised to "George Washington Parke Custis, the grandson of my wife and to his heirs the tract I hold on four mile run in the vicinity of Alexandria containing one thousand two hundred acres more or less and my entire square No. 21 in the City of Washington."

It is a curious fact that although Square No. 21 and most of the Four Mile Run tract were in 1799 located in the District of Columbia, the will passed no title to Square No. 21 but did pass title to the Four Mile Run tract. This was because the will was holographic, wholly in the handwriting of the testator, but not witnessed. Such a will passed no title to land in that part of the District ceded by Maryland, but did pass title in the part given by Virginia. At Washington's death Custis was still a minor. He continued to live at Mount Vernon until the death of Martha Washington in 1802, when he commenced the erection of Arlington Mansion. In 1805 he married Mary Fitzhugh, the daughter of Thomas Fitzhugh of Ravensworth and lived at Arlington until his death in 1857.

During Custis' ownership the Four Mile Run tract came to be generally known as "Washington Forest" and is so styled in deeds made by Custis and G. W. Custis Lee, his successor in title. The delinquent tax list of Arlington

---

[41] Travels through North America. p. 202.

County for 1932 shows the name is still in use, for it lists for sale "30 acres in Washington Forest."

In 1836 Custis built a water grist mill on Four Mile Run.[42] The mill dam and mill race are still in use and now serve an ice plant on Columbia Turnpike. Custis' mill was called Arlington Mill. Later, when the railroad from Alexandria to Leesburg was built, it followed the valley of Four Mile Run along the border of the Custis tract, and the station located at the crossing of the turnpike was named Arlington. How much of the tract Custis had left when he died does not appear. The land records of Arlington and Fairfax show conveyances by him of about 200 acres; but the general indexes of deeds of Fairfax County contain references to other deeds by Custis recorded in books now destroyed. If these lost deeds conveyed portions of the tract they must have been at the southern end— the part that George Mason called "mean," as there are no subsisting records showing deeds for this southern part comprising about 400 acres either from Custis, or Custis Lee who succeeded to his title.

The will of George Washington Parke Custis, dated March 26, 1855, devised to his "daughter and only child, Mary Ann Randolph Lee, my Arlington House estate containing eleven hundred acres and my mill on Four Mile Run in the County of Alexandria and the lands of mine adjacent to said mill in the counties of Alexandria and Fairfax . . . during the term of her natural life" and on her death the same was devised "to my eldest grandson Geo. Washington Custis Lee and his heirs forever, he, my eldest grandson taking my name and arms."[43]

Custis died in 1857 and his daughter, Mrs. Robert E. Lee, died in 1873.

George Washington Custis Lee entered the Confederate Army and rose to the rank of a major-general. He succeeded his father in the Presidency of Washington and

[42] Deed Book, Arlington Co., W–2, p. 184.
[43] Arlington Co. Wills Book.

Lee University. Very naturally he preferred to retain the illustrious name of Lee, and to safeguard his title both to Arlington and to the Four Mile Run tract, from possible divesture by his failure to fulfill the condition that he should assume the Custis name and arms, he procured a release from his brothers and sisters. [44]

In the year 1880 G. W. Custis Lee of Lexington, Virginia, conveyed to J. W. Barcroft, 62 acres on the west side of Four Mile Run, part of Washington Forest. [45] This was the Custis mill tract. Barcroft tore down the Custis mill and built another where the Columbia Turnpike crosses Four Mile Run, which he named after himself. The name of the railroad station was also changed to its present name of Barcroft.

Besides his conveyance to Barcroft, General Custis Lee sold about 400 acres in small parcels ranging from two to fifty acres during the period from 1880 to 1890 and laid off an outlet road for their convenience. The $150,000 he received as the consideration of his conveyance of the Arlington estate to the United States put him in comfortable circumstances, and on August 29, 1898, he made a deed of gift of what remained of the tract three, parcels aggregating 325 acres, to the Trustees of the Protestant Episcopal Seminary and High School in Virginia. [46] They still own parts of these tracts.

Custis Lee also gave to the Trustees of the Seminary, Washington's rough notes of one of his surveys of the tract, written on the back of a letter of introduction to him given by Patrick Henry to a young man. [47] This letter I am informed is now at Mount Vernon.

---

[44] D. B. Arlington Co., Liber B-4, folio 414.
[45] D. B. Arlington Co., Liber E-4, folio 279.
[46] D. B. Arlington Co., Vol. 4, p. 303.
[47] Prussing—Estate of George Washington deceased.

SIMON PEARSON'S PATENTS

The Pearson family of Stafford County played a leading part in the patenting and seating of the land along Four Mile Run. A survey of the Virginia shore of the Potomac River made in 1741 shows an island south of Four Mile Run estuary styled "Pearson's Island". There is no such island today. The place is a headland on the river with low ground behind, and adjoins the railroad freight yard. The new Mount Vernon boulevard passes through it. The name has disappeared from modern maps and is all but forgotten. It is believed to go back to the end of the seventeenth century when some member of the Pearson family occupied it as a tenant of Robert Alexander, but the name shows that the Pearsons were among the earliest settlers or occupants of the neighborhood. Two members of the family, Thomas, and his son, Simon, patented tracts on or near the run, aggregating 4000 acres, besides other tracts in the vicinity.

The scanty facts as to the early history of this family in Virginia are contained in a notice in the William and Mary College Quarterly. [1] One Thomas Pierson is said to have come to Virginia from the Isle of Ely before 1639 and to have married in Virginia, Susanna, sister of Theodorick Bland of Westover. Nothing more is known of him, but from the fact that the name Susanna appears repeatedly in the Pearson line, and that Theodorick Bland, nephew of the first Theodorick and a Thomas Pearson were living in Stafford County in the late seventeenth century, it is believed that the Pearsons of Stafford and Fairfax counties are descended from Thomas Pierson and Susanna, his wife. Very little remains of the early Stafford records. Between the immigrant Thomas Pierson and the Thomas Pearson

---

[1] Vol. 10–65.

who patented land on Four Mile Run in the early eighteenth century, there is a missing generation. From the custom of naming the eldest son after the father, it is conjectured that Thomas Pierson and Susanna his wife, had a son Thomas, who settled in Stafford. This son, whatever his name, left at least two children, Susanna and Thomas. Susanna married Major John West of Stafford who died before 1698, leaving her surviving. Thomas Pearson, the third of the name, is probably the one whose name became attached to the island below Four Mile Run. In 1706 he, and three associates, John West, William Harrison and Thomas Harrison, took out a patent for 4639 acres [2] on the south side of Hunting Creek, west of John Mathews patent. It is often referred to as the Harrison patent.

In 1707 he received a patent for 660 acres on the south side of Four Mile Run [3] which included the land opposite Bluemont Junction and extended south to include Munson Hill. The lost Stafford records probably contained more information about him. The Northern Neck Land Grants show no more patents to him. He probably died soon after 1707. A later patent of 1730 adjoined the "land of Thomas Pearson, deceased". He left issue a son Simon and may have left other children. About this son, "Capt. Simon Pearson", a little more information is available. Between 1724 and 1731, either by himself, or in conjection with others, he took out seven patents for land situated in the present Fairfax and Arlington counties. Four of them were on or near Four Mile Run. The first issued in 1724 [4] comprised 1279 acres at the head waters of Pimmit and the branch of Holmes run now called Tripps. This large tract included the western half of the town of Falls Church and extended for two miles. One of its eastern lines ran close to the spot where the Falls Church now stands, though the church itself is built on land patented by Michael Reagan. In 1726 Simon Pearson and John Fitzhugh patented 1209

---

[2] N.N., 3–225.

[3] N.N., A–57.

[4] N.N., A–57.

acres on the middle run, commonly called the horse pen of Great Hunting Creek. This land lay between Falls Church and Ravensworth.[5] In 1729 Pearson patented 330 acres on the southerly Long Branch of Four Mile Run. It includes the present Baileys Cross-roads.[6] Its subsequent history will be traced later in this paper. In 1730 Simon Pearson and James Going took out a grant for 650 acres on the north side of Four Mile Run[7] which included the present subdivision of Fostoria. In 1731 Pearson and Gabriel Adams received a patent for 708 acres north of Falls Church, running "Back to Brandymore Castle" which seems to have been the first name of Minor's Hill.[8] Another of his patents not far away was for 231 acres on the Timber Branch of Great Hunting Creek.[9] Another smaller patent for 195 acres near the Potomac river on the hills between Rosslyn and Chain Bridge was issued to him in 1729.[10] He also acquired by purchase two tracts from James Robertson, situated on the northerly Long Branch of Four Mile Run, and inherited from his father the 660 acre tract at Bluemont Junction mentioned above.

Virginia colonial legislation required that all tobacco for export be brought to public warehouses for inspection. The inspection act of 1732 recites that such a warehouse had been built on the upper side of Great Hunting Creek on the land of Simon Pearson.[11] This was his Timber Branch patent which lay on the north side of Hunting Creek estuary, just west of the Alexandria Cemetery a little below

---

[5] N.N., B–34. John Fitzhugh was a son of Col. William Fitzhugh of "Bedford" Stafford County who had patented the huge Ravensworth tract in 1694. The tract on the horse pen of Hunting Creek was subsequently petitioned by the Pearson and Fitzhugh heirs. See plat in Survey Book of Fairfax County 1742-1765.

[6] N.N., C–27.

[7] N.N., C–118.

[8] N.N., D–40.

[9] N.N., C–25.

[10] N.N., C–28.

[11] 4th Henning's Statutes p. 311.

the ford of the creek. Timber Branch is now called Hoof's Run, though the original name is still applied to a branch of Hoof's Run. The warehouse could not have continued there long, as Berry's survey of the Howsing patent made seven years later does not show such a warehouse. It shows only "Hugh West's Hunting Creek warehouse" on the Potomac river front within the present City of Alexandria. It wâs probably found advisable to shift the warehouse to the deeper waterfront on the river.

Simon Pearson was married twice, but the name of his first wife is not known. His second wife, was Hannah Ball, widow of RaleighTravers and daughter of Col. Joseph Ball, of Epping Forest. She was a sister of Washington's mother. His issue was all by his first marriage. His second wife survived him and lived until 1748.

Capt. Simon Pearson was a man of some prominence and wealth. ˙ He lived in Overwharton parish, in Stafford County. As his will was proved in the court of that county in 1733, which was after Prince William County had been formed, he must have lived south of Chappawamsic Creek, probably not far from Aquia church. The record of his will has fortunately survived. It is dated December 3d, 1731.[12] It gives to his wife Hannah, the use of certain negroes for her life; to his daughter Constantia, and the heirs of her body 432 acres of land in Prince William County "which I bought of James Robertson according to the metes and bounds mentioned in the Proprietor's Office", with negroes; to his daughter Susanna and the heirs of her body 195 acres "which I bought of James Robertson[13] adjoining the 432 acres devised to my daughter Constantia"; also "330 acres on the south branch of Four Mile Run and the branches of Great Hunting Creek

[12] Stafford county records, M–111.
[13] For James Robertson's patents see page 7. Simon Pearson's purchases of Robertson were at the north end of the latter's patents "Chapman's Quarter" on Berry's plat of the Howsing patent shows their location.

in Prince William County, according to the bounds mentioned in the deed from the Proprietor's Office of the 17th of February 1729, and negroes": to his daughter "Margaret and the heirs of her body all that tract of land bought of Capt. Thomas Harrison on the branches of Great Hunting Creek; also 213 acres on Timber Branch, according to the bounds mentioned in the deed from the Proprietor's Office of the 17th of February, 1729", and negroes: To his son Thomas, and the heirs of his body all the rest of his lands, and negroes:

"I give what money I have in England remaining due me, after goods I have sent for are paid for ....to purchase negroes for my daughters, Susanna and Margaret; wearing apparel sent for to be divided between my wife and children; gold rings and trunk to each daughter. All other personal property to be divided between my wife, son and daughters.

"Son Thomas to have the care and tuition of daughters Susanna and Margaret, until they shall attain eighteen years or be married, and he shall in such management pursue and follow the advice of Capt. Thomas Harrison."

The will named as executors the testator's wife, his daughter Constantia and his son Thomas. "My good friend Thomas Harrison [14] to be coadjutor and assistant to them". Among the witnesses to the will were John Mercer of Marlborough and the Rev. Alexander Scott, rector of Overwharton Parish, whose seat was at Dipple on the Potomac, south of Chappawamsic Creek, where his tombstone is still preserved.

---

[14] Capt. Thomas Harrison (1665–1746) was a son of Burr Harrison who had been a burgess from Stafford in the late 17th century, and a pioneer on Chappawamsic. Thomas, of the text was Sheriff of Prince William in 1732, and like his father, lived on Chappawamsic Creek. In 1718 he sold to Simon Pearson 289 acres out of his share in the tract of 4639 acres on Great Hunting Creek, patented in 1706 by Thomas Pearson, John West, William and Thomas Harrison (see recital in Prince William D. B., E–355,) and this land Simon Pearson devised to his daughter Margaret.

The will was evidently drawn by a lawyer, and presumably by John Mercer. The limitations to the heirs of the body of each of the devisees created estates tail. Each devise was followed by a cross limitation in tail to one or more of the other children, on the failure of heirs of the body of the first tenant in tail; with an ultimate limitation over to the testator's right heirs on the extinction of the issue of all the four children. As it happened, all four had issue living in 1776 when the system of entails was abolished. The will was in the approved English form of strict settlement, except that it conferred no power on the tenants in tail to execute leases extending beyond their own lives.

The inventory shows that in addition to his home plantation, Pearson had two quarters in the part of Prince William now in Fairfax and Arlington Counties. At the upper quarter which was probably the "Chapman's Quarter", shown on Berry's survey, were negro slaves, a considerable quantity of farm implements, stock and between five and six thousand pounds of tobacco.

When Simon Pearson died, Stafford was no longer a frontier county. A small land and slave owning gentry was emerging and controlled its political and social life. Pearson's neighbors and associates included the Fitzhughs of Bedford, Marmion and Eagles Nest, the Thorntons of Society Hill; the Daniels of Crow's Nest; the Seldens of Salvington; the Alexanders of Caledon and Salisbury, the Brents of Woodstock and Richland; the Waughs of Belle Plaine; the Mercers of Marlborough; the Lees of Bellevue and Berry Hill; the Peytons of Stony Hill and Tusculum; the Hedgmans of the Cottage; the Harrisons of Chappawamsic; the Strothers, Travers, Mountjoys and Doniphans. Like many of its neighbors the Pearson family possessed a coat of arms.

Simon Pearson was a member of this nascent aristocracy, and his will and his patents show his plans for the future of his family. He had concentrated his grants and his purchases in the Four Mile and Hunting Creek neighborhood. While his will entailed all land passing under it, the

69

parcels given the daughters were small. The bulk of the estate was entailed on the only son Thomas, with the expectation that he would move to this new locality and build up a great estate to be transmitted to future generations of the Pearson name. He did not foresee the coup de grace that Thomas Jefferson would deal to his schemes half a century later. The land that had descended to Simon Pearson from his father also passed by the will to Thomas Pearson, so that the latter must have gotten by the will upwards of 5000 acres in the valleys of Four Mile Run and Great Hunting Creek.

Of the daughters named (the fifth generation in Virginia), the eldest, Constantia, was born in 1714. Before her father's death she married Nathaniel Chapman[15] and survived until 1791. Susanna was born in 1717; married John Alexander on December 11th, 1734; survived him and died October 6th, 1788; Margaret was born March 5th, 1720, and died in 1796.[16] She married, first, William Henry Terrett, and second, her cousin Col. John West. Her second husband made more of a stir in the world than her first, as he was a vestryman of Truro parish, a burgess from Fairfax, and a merchant in Alexandria. Each of these daughters gave one of her sons the christian name of Pearson, and Susanna named another son Simon.

The son, Thomas, was the oldest child. He fulfilled his father's expectation that he would make his home on the land devised to him. He was a resident of Truro parish (then in Prince William county) in 1740. He was a justice of the Prince William court, and on the organization of Fairfax County in 1742, he was made a justice of the court of that county.[17] He built a house and resided on the 1279 acre tract patented by his father in 1724. The evidence is a survey of the tract made in 1765 recorded in the first Fairfax survey book, page 40, which shows "house

---

[15] See end of this paper for note on the Chapman family.
[16] These dates are from William and Mary Quarterly, 10–14.
[17] Old Prince William Landmarks, p 321.

70

where Capt. Thomas Pearson, deceased, formerly lived". It was located about two miles west of the Falls Church, and near the road leading to "old court house" and Difficult run. As late as 1880 an old dormered house with a sweeping roof, evidently dating from the early eighteenth century, stood near the Alexandria and Leesburg pike, south of the road and not far from Pimmitt run. An enormous English boxwood bush overshadowed the rear of the house. The location was near the spot indicated on the old plat as the house of Capt. Thomas Pearson, and it is likely that they were identical.

In 1740 and 1741 Thomas Pearson leased 150 and 100 acres on Four Mile Run for three lives to Henry Collum and John Hurst respectively.[18] They were apparently carved out of the Munson Hill tract patented by his grandfather. He knew that as tenant in tail, his leases would not bind his successors; and was careful to recite the fact in the leases. Leases for three lives have fallen into disuse at the present time, but they were common in Virginia in the eighteenth century. These leases named the usual lessees, the tenant, his wife and a son of the tenant. The purpose of such leases was to get the land seated, cleared and cultivated, reserving rent and the reversion to the lessor and his heirs. From the tenant's standpoint, they were not attractive propositions. A man who farmed land wanted to own it absolutely.

The Northern Neck land grants show a single patent to this Thomas Pearson, issued in 1742, for 1018 acres on Beaverdam in Prince William (now Loudoun county).[19] In 1742 waste and ungranted tracts of a thousand acres were becoming scarce anywhere in old Prince William.

Thomas Pearson married a daughter of John Markham. He died while still a comparatively young man, certainly not 40 and probably not over 35 years of age. His will dated December 7th, 1743 was proved in the Fairfax

---

[18] Prince William D.B., E 97 and 436.
[19] N.N., E-458.

County Court.[20] It names two daughters, Eliza and Margaret, to each of whom a negro man was given when they attained lawful age, or married. To Hugh West he devised a tract of land at Rankin's Point ("that was formerly Conoy's Island"). This land, in the river opposite Loudoun County had been conveyed to him by West, probably on secret trust. The remainder of his estate he directed should be equally divided between his wife and the rest of his children not before mentioned. The daughter Eliza, or Elizabeth married in 1756 Allan Macrea,[21] the Scotch merchant of Dumfries, and their daughter Amelia married her cousin, George Chapman (see note 15). Thomas Pearson left two sons, Simon and Thomas, both minors. The land their father held as tenant in tail was not affected by the will, and vested in tail in the elder son, Simon. Both sons lived their lives in Fairfax county and made their homes on the Alexandria and Leesburg road near the Falls Church. In 1745 William Henry Terrett, their uncle was appointed guardian of Simon Pearson.[22]

---

[20] Fairfax Wills, A–15.

[21] Compendium of American Genealogy, 5–162.

[22] Fairfax Wills Book A page 140. The Terretts were among the early settlers in this part of Virginia. The William Henry Terrett mentioned, was named deputy clerk of Fairfax County on its organization. In 1741 he patented 982 acres lying between Great Hunting Creek and the existing Seminary road, adjoining the Mercer tract that Washington bought (N.N., E–412) and in 1746 another parcel of 127 acres next to his first patent (N.N., F–251) and in the same year acquired 300 acres from Gabriel Adams "Adjoining the land of Parson Scott and Thomas Harrison (Fairfax D.B., B–13). As above stated he married Margaret, daughter of Simon Pearson, who survived him. He had issue, sons Pearson (who died without issue in his father's lifetime), William Henry Terrett, Jr., Nathaniel Terrett and other children. His will dated February 7th, 1755, proved in 1758 (Fairfax Wills B–185) gave to his son William Henry his home plantation of 1000 acres, provided he made over to "the child my wife now goes with, if it be a boy, the land whereon John Summers now dwells". His widow married her cousin John West, and survived him. Her will

72

In 1759 shortly after attaining his majority Simon Pearson conveyed to his brother Thomas 500 acres on the branches of Four Mile Run" on which land Philip Saunders now lives as a tenant". The consideration is recited to be natural love and affection and also "for and toward the better support, maintenance and livelihood of said Thomas."[23] I am not able to identify this land.

In 1762 he gave to John Hurst a confirmatory lease for the land on Four Mile Run, this time for the lives of Hurst's three children, Sybil, William and Jean, and the longest liver of them.[24] As Simon Pearson outlived the abolition of entails, the lease was effective for the lives of the lessees.

In 1760 he had a transaction with Washington, a notice of which is preserved in the diaries.

"April 15, 1760. Being informed that French, Triplett and others were about buying a piece of land of Simon Pearson's, lying not far from my Dogue Run Quarter, I engaged him to give me the first offer of it so soon as he should determine on selling it."[25] As the land was en-

---

proved in 1798 (Fairfax Wills G–329) shows a considerable landed estate and mentions children William Henry Terrett, Nathaniel Terrett, Constant Washington, Anna Powell, Susanna Terrett and Roger West (her son by her second marriage), besides grandchildren. The second William Henry Terrett married Amelia, daughter of Nathaniel Chapman Hunter, lived his whole life on his fathers patent, and survived until 1826. His will mentions his wife Amelia, sons, George Hunter Terrett and John Hunter Terrett, and daughter Nancy Douglas Macrea, wife of Allan Macrea (Fairfax Wills, O–136).

[23] Fairfax D.B., D–606.

[24] Fairfax D.B., D–903.

[25] Diaries 1–155. This may have been part of the West, Harrison and Pearson patent of 1706 (see note 2). There is evidence that the tract was partitioned among the patentees. Thomas Pearson's share descended to his son, the first Simon, who entailed all his estate. Washington subsequently sold the land to Lund Washington and it was probably part of the latter's Hayfield estate.

73

tailed the sale was consummated by a writ ad quod damnum, a survey, a view and verdict of a jury, and a deed recorded in general court of the province. The sale and conveyance of the 178 acres involved therefore does not appear on the Fairfax land records. Washington was to hear more of the matter after he retired from public life.

In 1784 Carlyle Fairfax Whiting added to the extensive estate he had acquired by the will of his grandfather John Carlyle, sixty-seven acres near the Falls Church by purchase from Simon Pearson. It was contiguous to land he already owned. [26]

The indexes of the lost books of Fairfax show many other conveyances to and from Simon Pearson, as was to be expected from his large holdings. Sometime before 1760 he married Milkey, the daughter of John Trammell. [27] "Unhappy differences" soon led to a separation agreement and property settlement.

There was a John Pearson living near the Alexandria and Leesburg road in the late 18th century, in whose welfare Simon Pearson took such a warm interest as to suggest that he may have been a natural son. The Fairfax order book, September court, 1789 gives the names of the tithables ordered to work on the road from the widow Tuckers to Falls Church. The names are set down in the approximate order of residences from east to west. Simon Pearson

---

[26] Fairfax D.B., O–246.

[27] Milkey Trammell was the daughter of John Trammell and Susanna, his wife. In 1733 Alexander Scott conveyed to John and Susanna Trammell of Truro parish 200 acres near Pimmit Run (Pr. Wm. D.B. B–136). The will of John Trammell was proved in 1755 in the Fairfax county court, and names sons, William, Sampson, John and daughters Betty Hickman, Lettice Orford (Offutt?), Susan Trammell and Milkey Trammell. Milkey is evidently a free rendering of the biblical Milcah. Sampson Trammell was living in 1784 two miles west of the Falls Church where Washington and Dr. Craik stopped for dinner on the journey to Washington's western lands (Dairies 2–279). Representatives of this family still live in northern Fairfax.

and John Pearson were apparently living in the same house or close together, while Thomas Pearson was living in a different neighborhood. By two deeds made in 1786 and 1796[28] Simon Pearson conveyed land on the Leesburg Road, west of Falls Church in trust for Peletiah Graffort for life, and in remainder to her son, John Pearson. The deed recites that this land was part of a larger tract "granted by the Proprietors of the Northern Neck unto Simon Pearson, father of him, said Simon to whom it descended." The patent referred to was the one issued in 1724 for 1279 acres at the head of Tripps, Pimmit, and Four Mile Runs, but the statement that Simon Pearson, the elder, was the father of Simon Pearson, the younger, is incomprehensible. Father is surely a scrivener or copyist's error for grandfather.

Simon Pearson died in the spring of 1797, and by his will made in 1786,[29] and proved in 1798 devised all estate to his brother Thomas. He had not been dead six months, when Thomas brought suit as "heir in tail" to Simon to set aside the inquisition and deed by which Washington acquired the 178 acres near his Dogue Run Quarter.

Washington retained Bushrod Washington to defend the suit, in an interesting letter printed in Ford's edition of his writings[30] in which he mooted the sensible point whether the act of the Virginia Assembly, abolishing entails had not cured the alleged irregularities in the proceedings by which the land had passed from Pearson to him. Some years later the Court of Appeals of Virginia decided that irregularities in conveyances in fee made by tenants tail before the statute of 1776 were validated by that in act.[31] The letter also contained this cryptic sentence: "3d;

---

[28] Fairfax D.B., X–5, Z–435. (This John Pearson married Sarah Follin (or Fallen) in 1782.)

[29] Fairfax Wills G p.

[30] Writings 13–422.

[31] Orndorf vs Turman, 2 Leigh 200.

Whether as Simon was lawfully married and never divorced, the children of that woman, though begotten no matter by whom in the state of separation from him, is not a bar to the claim of Thomas?" — Which shows that for all his absence on public business, Washington kept himself passably informed of the current Fairfax gossip.

There is more on the Fairfax records about the troubles of Simon and Milkey Pearson. A solution by divorce was not so simple, as Washington's remark would imply. Before the Revolution and for some years after, a divorce could be gotten only by a private act of the Assembly. From the old records one can piece together the story at which the letter hinted. It is the story of Simon Pearson's down fall. First, there are the reports of his guardian. They give a picture of the young heir's education, his clothes, his horses, his slaves, his rents. With his influential connections, and his large landed estate, the way seemed open to a seat in the county court or perhaps in the House of Burgesses. About 1760 came his early marriage to a young woman a little beneath him socially; then in less than two years a separation. The mismated couple wasted no time over an impossible divorce. They parted and each, apparently formed a new connection. Some years later Simon setled land in trust for a girl still lower in the social scale, daughter of a tavern keeper. The second union, however, proved lasting. Toward the end of his life he conveyed his dwelling, his plantation, his furniture, his cattle and horses to his companion for her life and in remainder to "her son", to whom he gave his own name. He dies, an old man, leaving to his brother Thomas, what is left. But the discarded wife has the last word. In 1806 the aged Miicah Pearson widow of Simon Pearson, conveyed to John T. Pearson "only son and child living of said Simon Pearson and said Milcah Pearson" her dower interest in all those tracts which said Simon had conveyed away without her knowledge or joinder.[32] The deed was

---

[32] Fairfax D.B., G 2–123.

her vindication from aspersions such as Washington hinted
at. The dower was incidental. What Simon's aristo-
cratic aunts, Col. West's lady, and the widows Chapman
and Alexander, thought of their wilful and defiant nephew
no yellowed page tells.

The Fairfax records do not show how long Thomas
Pearson survived his brother. There are many Pearsons
in northern Virginia today. It is believed that they descend from Thomas Pearson. The name Smon has been
preserved in the female line as Simonetta.

THE BAILEYS CROSS ROADS TRACT

On February 17th, 1729 there was issued in the name
of the fifth Lord Fairfax a patent to Capt. Simon Pearson,
for a tract in Stafford County recited to contain 330 acres
on the southern branch of Four Mile Run, subsequently
called Long Branch. It might well have been called the
Long Branch tract for it included all that stream except
its source and its mouth. Here it may be noticed that
short as Four Mile Run is, it has two Long Branches. The
other flows southerly along the west boundary of the
Howsing patent, and has been several times mentioned in
that connection. In early deeds it was styled the northerly Long Branch of Four Mile Run to distinguish it from
the Long Branch running through the Pearson patent.
The road leading from Hunting Creek warehouse to Difficult run was the only road through the tract, and was probably a rude trail as early as 1729.

Simon Pearson died four years after getting the patent.
His will devised it to his young daughter, Susanna, describing it as "330 acres on the south branch of Four Mile Run
and the branches of Great Hunting Creek in Prince William County bought from the Proprietor's Office February
17, 1729". As stated, she married John Alexander. The
tract thereafter took the name of her husband. When
Moses Ball got his grant in 1748 his south boundary was

described as the north line of Alexander's land. I am unable to say whether John Alexander ever had tenants on the land. The land in the vicinity later acquired by Washington bordered the Pearson patent for a mile and a quarter, but the indications from the Diaries are that as late as 1786, the dividing line betwen the tracts ran through woodland. Other parts of the Alexander tract may, of course, have been under cultivation. When he married, John Alexander was living on Pearson's island, but he soon returned to the Alexander home of Caledon in what was then Stafford county. He is usually styled John Alexander of Chotank. He died in Stafford in 1766 and the chances are his widow, Susanna, returned to Fairfax, as it is known that her eldest son Charles and most of her other children resided there.

By deed dated October 8th, 1773 Susanna Alexander conveyed the whole tract to John Luke. The deed was not recorded in Fairfax county. Under the terms of her father's will, she was tenant in tail, and the Act of Assembly of 1748 required that the necessary proceedings enabling a tenant in tail to convey in fee simple be certified to the office of the Secretary of Colony, and the deed recorded in the General Court at Williamsburg. A later conveyance recites that it was so recorded.

John Luke apparently took possession of the land and seems to have lived upon it, as he (or his son of the same name) was present when Washington made his last survey of his own adjoining land in 1799. [33]

The elder John Luke seems to come to Virginia from elsewhere as he made a certificate that his removal to Virginia was with no intent of evadng the laws against further importation of slaves; that he brought no slaves with him with intent to sell them; that none of his slaves had been imported from the West Indies since November 1, 1778. [34]

---

[33] Washington's Diaries, 4 p 301.
[34] Fairfax D.B., V-296.

78

There is no will of John Luke. As the Fairfax general indexes of deeds are preserved in their entirety, although particular deed books are missing, and as they show no deed from the elder Luke to the younger, the gift must have been by a will recorded elsewhere.

Early in the 19th century while the Lukes owned the tract, the Columbia turnpike was opened through it. Contemporary deeds call it the "Washington Gravelled Road".[35] The intersection of this road with the old Leesburg road created a cross road, which the subsequent opening of the new (present) Leesburg road converted into a junction of five forks. As a good part of the road lay within Alexandria County, then in the District of Columbia, a charter was obtained from Congress authorizing the formation of a stock company to build a road from the Causeway leading from Alexander's Island to the boundary of the District of Columbia in the most direct and practicable route toward the Little River Turnpike.[36] It was a toll road and charges were levied not only for vehicles but for droves of cattle, sheep and pigs.....................which it was expected would be driven over it to the markets of the new City of Washington.

In 1798 John Luke put a mortgage on the tract which recited that it had been patented to Simon Pearson for 330 acres, but contained by actual measurement 580 acres and devised by him to his daughter Susanna who by the name of Susanna Alexander had conveyed the same by deed recorded in the general court of Virginia to John Luke, father of the John Luke who made this mortgage.[37]

The mortgage was foreclosed by a chancery suit in the County Court of Fairfax and the property was sold and conveyed by Edmund Jennings Lee and others, commissioners, to William B. Randolph of Washington City, who sold off small lots to Lawrence Lacy and Wesley Adams.

---

[35] Arlington Co. D.B., 2-537.

[36] 2 Statutes at Large 570.

[37] Fairfax D.B., A 2-450.

The balance he conveyed in 1837 to Hachaliah Bailey of Westchester, N. Y.[38] The deed contained a new description based upon a survey. Its beginning point was near the present Hummer house on the road opened by John and Moses Ball from the Leesburg turnpike to their farms where the village of Glencarlyn now is. In 1837, according to the deed, there was a school house near this beginning point. The northern boundary of the tract ran from thence east for a mile along the southerly line of Moses Ball's patent, crossing Long Branch not far from its confluence with Four Mile Run. Certain of its eastern and southern lines ran with the lines of the Gabriel Adams patent, which once belonged to Washington and was then owned by George W. P. Custis. The road junction, now Bailey's Cross Roads was in the southeast part of the tract. In 1843 Hachaliah Bailey deeded the land to Mariah Bailey, wife of Lewis Bailey of Fairfax County.[39]

The Baileys built a large frame house, a portion of which still stands. Before the Civil War they had an inn and a store at the cross roads, and did a large dairy business. Later the inn was moved from the cross roads to the homestead, and the huge building became a well known boarding house. Mrs. Bailey was fond of flowers and had a small conservatory. In the yard were many shrubs, althea, crepe myrtle, spirea, forsythias, lilacs, and hardy roses. Long Branch flowed near the house, and was dammed to make a small pond stocked wth fish.[40]

The Civil War brought many vicissitudes to the neighborhood. During the summer of 1861 the Confederate Cavalry under Col. J. E. B. Stuart occupied Munson Hill, while the Federal outposts were at Bailey's Cross Roads. There was frequent skirmishing and occasional casualties until September 28th when McClellan advanced his lines three miles. The northern soldiers cut through

---

[38] Fairfax D.B., D 2–395.

[39] Fairfax D.B., H 3–192.

[40] Article by John Claggett Proctor in the Washington Star, February 27, 1929.

the banks of the Bailey pond and drained the water to get the fish. In a field adjoining the house President Lincoln reviewed McClellan's army in November, 1861. The soldiers tore down the fences to build a grandstand for President Lincoln, his cabinet, General McClellan and distinguished guests. The Baileys were compensated by Congress for the damage done to the property. Julia Ward Howe was one of the spectators and her "Battle Hymn of the Republic" was written the morning after she had witnessed the stirring scene. Sherman's army camped on the same farm in 1865 before taking part in the grand review.

The Baileys sold off a number of farms and tracts, one of which is now owned by the writer of this sketch. They also sold sites for a church and a school house. A portion of the Bailey house was moved about a quarter of of a mile and is now the property of Mr. Charles F. Miller. Mrs. Bailey died in 1895 and the remainder of the tract was subdivided by order of the Circuit Court of Fairfax County (Anthony W. Armstrong and R. Walton Moore, Commissioners); all the subdivisions except the homestead being allotted to the heirs. The homestead was sold in 1897 to J. Millard Moore, assistant Commissioner of Patents, who has made the central part his summer home for many years. He made no attempt to repair or restore the whole house, and has recently taken down all not used by him for a residence. A small part of the tract is still owned by and occupied by one of the Bailey heirs.

THE CHAPMAN FAMILY OF FAIRFAX COUNTY

Jonathan Chapman and his son, Nathaniel, settled on Four Mile Run in the early 18th century. Nathaniel married Constantia Pearson before the death of her father, Simon Pearson, in 1733. Her brother Thomas Pearson in 1732 acquired a tract of 150 acres, a part of the Howsing patent, situated on the north bank of Four Mile Run estuary at its junction with the Potomac River. (Deeds of

81

lease and release Pr. Wm. D.B., B–1 & 2). I can find no deed from him to either Jonathan or Nathaniel Chapman, but it is certain the Chapmans took possession of the tract shortly after then, claiming the ownership through him. Berry's survey of 1741 shows "Mr. Chapman's house" there.

The Northern Neck land grants (F–80) show Jonathan Chapman as patenting 650 acres on Broad Run next to Col. Carter's land in 1742. This was at the Thoroughfare Gap of the Bull Run Mountains where the well known Chapman Mill was afterward built. In 1749 Nathaniel Chapman patented 699 acres on the north side of Pignut Mountain (N.N., G–151) near his father's land, and he had other patents. Moses Ball stated that Nathaniel Chapman purchased land further up Four Mile Run from the devisees of Evans Thomas. The tract at the mouth of Four Mile Run was given the name of Summer Hill and remained in the family for more than a century.

Nathaniel Chapman was a charter member of the Ohio Company, and had experience in iron making at the Principio iron mines in Maryland, and the Accokeek mines in Virginia. Washington's Diaries testify to his reputation as an iron master. A foot note by the editor (Diaries 1–138) states that he was executor of the estates of Augustine and Lawrence Washington. Later he moved to Charles County, Maryland. He died in 1760 intestate in Baltimore County, apparently while on business connected with the iron works there. The inventory of his estate (Fairfax Wills, B–333) shows he had land in Prince William, Fairfax, Fauquier and Loudoun counties as well as in Maryland.

His widow Constantia (or Constant, as she called herself) lived until 1791. When her husband died she was in Charles County, but returned to Fairfax about 1770 with her son George. She seems to have lived at Summer Hill. She was a woman of refinement and education, and an intimate friend of the Mason family of Gunston. Copies of her will and codicil survive in a mutilated condition (Fairfax Wills, F–1 and G–361). She devised the residue of her estate to her son George. The first two pages of the copy of the will in G–361 are missing from that book but a copy of the whole will was preserved among the papers of one her descendants, the late Fanny B. Hunter of Alexandria. This portion of the will has been recently printed in a book on the Hunter Family by Sidney Mathiot Culbertson of Denver to whom I am indebted for it, as also for information about Constant Chapman's Hunter descendants set out below. The missing portion of the will is:

"In the Name of God, Amen.

I, Constant Chapman of Charles County, in the Province of Maryland, widow and relict of Nathaniel Chapman, Gent, do make this my last will and testament.

I direct my executors to build a vault fronting on the creek in the square of the garden opposite the graves on the old plantation at Four Mile Creek, in Fairfax County, where I formerly lived, in which vault I desire my body to be deposited, and also the bodys of my children, and such other of my relatives as there are buried, and as to the remains of Mr. Chapman, my late husband's father (who lies buried in the same place) I leave it to the discretion of my sons and daughters whether the same shall be interred in the vault or not.

I direct my executors to erect a tombstone over my late husband who lies buried in Baltimore County, Maryland, inscribed with his age and the time of his death.

I give and bequeath unto my daughter Elizabeth Hunter, 100 pounds current money of Virginia in trust to be laid out in the education of her children in such manner as she thinks proper.

I also give and bequeath carriages, harness, horses and cattle..........

I give and bequeath unto each of my three grandchildren viz. Nathaniel Chapman Weems, James William Locke Weems and Sarah Louisa Weems the sum of five guineas to be laid out for them in silver plate; as their mother shall think proper, said plate to be engraved with the arms of the Chapman and Pearson familys. I give to

83

my eldest son, Pearson Chapman, a mourning ring of the value of one guinea and no more, he having inherited the greatest part of his father's estate; unto my friend Mrs. Ann Mason a mourning ring to·be set around with diamond sparks, the said ring to be the value of three guineas and a half, and be inscribed with my age and the time of my death".

This will was made on November 2d, 1768. Mrs. Ann Mason was the first wife of George Mason of Gunston and predeceased Constant Chapman by many years.

Though most of the bequests must have failed through changed conditions, the will is interesting for its information, and still more, for the light it sheds on the character of its author. It is the will of a woman conscious of her gentle blood and of her assured position in the society in which she lived.

The issue of the marriage of Nathaniel and Constant Chapman was three sons and three daughters. The sons were Nathaniel, Pearson and George. The eldest son, Nathaniel, was born in 1740 and died intestate and without issue shortly after his father. (Fairfax D.B., G–p–33). Pearson Chapman (1745–1784) lived in Charles County near Glymont and built the handsome Georgian house now known as Mount Aventine. Approached through a lane of poplars, the house overlooks a vast stretch of water. Washington visited the place. He "attempted to cross at the Widow Chapmans in order to pay Col. Mason a visit, but could not get over" (Diaries 3–132 November 31, 1786). A letter from George Mason to Pearson Chapman is printed in Rowland's Life of Mason (2–111). He married his cousin Susanna, daughter of John and Susanna Pearson Alexander. She was the "Widow Chapman" referred to.

By two deeds made in 1766 Pearson Chapman conveyed to his younger brother, George, two lots in Alexandria, and the 150 acre tract at the mouth of Four Mile Run, the latter being granted to "George Chapman and the heirs male of his body". (Fairfax D.B., G pages 33 and 35). Pearson Chapman's will was proved in Charles County. It mentions his wife, Susanna, sons Nathaniel, George and John, and "uncle John Chapman". Mt. Aventine remained in the family until the 20th century, and in 1873 its owner was another Pearson Chapman.

George Chapman, (born before 1750) was living in Charles County in 1766, but soon moved back to Summer Hill. In 1774 he married his cousin Amelia. She was the daughter of Allan McCrea, a wealthy Scotch merchant of Dumfries, by his wife Elizabeth Pearson McCrea.

The daughters of Nathaniel and Constant Chapman were Elizabeth, Amelia and Louisa. Elizabeth (born in 1733) married Dr. John Hunter, who came from Scotland, practiced medicine in Alexandria and died in 1763. Among the issue of this marriage was General John Chapman Hunter, whose seat was at "Contemplation" three miles north of Fairfax where he is buried, and Nathaniel Chapman Hunter, father of Alexander Hunter (1791–1849).

Amelia Chapman, second daughter of Nathaniel and Constant Chapman, married William Locke Weems (1735–1785) of Anne Arundel County, (American Compendium of Genealogy 5–714).

Louisa Chapman, the third daughter (born 1743) was the third wife of Washington's brother, Samuel. Her married life was spent in the lower Shenandoah Valley. There was no issue of their marriage.

George Chapman moved from Fairfax County to Prince William before 1800 and recited himself a resident of Fauquier County in 1802. He probably returned to Summer Hill as his will was proved in Alexandria County. He died in 1815 devising all his estate to his wife Amelia. She died after 1819 intestate.

The known children of George Chapman were three sons, George Chapman, Jr., Nathaniel Chapman and S. F. Chapman, (who resided in Washington City) and a daughter Louise, who married Alexander Hunter.

The second son Nathaniel was born at Summer Hill in 1780 and became a celebrated physician. After study-

ing medicine in London and in Edinburgh, he practiced in
Philadelphia. He was the editor of the Journal of Medical
and Physical Sciences and president of the American
Philosophical Society. He died in 1853.

Another descendant of Constant Chapman was John
Gadsby Chapman, born in Alexandria in 1808 and died in
Brooklyn in 1890. He was an artist and spent most of his
life in Itay. His best known work is "The Baptism of
Pocahontas" in the rotunda of the Capitol. Dr. Nathaniel
Chapman and John Gadsby Chapman descend from Simon
Pearson in a double line.

In 1802 George Chapman conveyed the Summer Hill
tract at the mouth of Four Mile Run to William Henry
Terrett (Arlington D.B., D-438) in trust for Amelia, the
wife of George, and on her death to sell and divide the proceeds among his children. Terrett never dealt with the
property.

In some way not shown by the record, probably by a
partition between the children of George Chapman, the
Summer Hill farm was assigned to Louise Chapman. In
1816 she married her cousin, Alexander Hunter, who purchased the adjoining Abingdon property. They lived at
Abingdon or at Summer Hill until Alexander Hunter died
in 1849. In 1851 Louise Hunter sold Summer Hill, which
so passed out of the Chapman family after an ownership of
125 years. Her deed of conveyance reserved the graveyard which is all that is left to testify to the former owners
of Summer Hill. It is in a clump of trees surrounded by a
rough wire fence. It overlooks the Potomac as far south
as Fort Foote, and the estuary of Four Mile Run, tranquil
and beautiful still, despite the causeways that stretch
across it. The vault that Constant Chapmans directed
her executors to build was never erected. The inscriptions
on the tombstones are:

"To Dr. John Hunter of Scotland who died in 1763
and Elizabeth Chapman his wife".

"In memory of Alexander Hunter, son of Nathaniel
C. and Sarah Ann Hunter; died January 21st, 1849, aged

58 years. He was 18 years U. S. Marshal of the District of Columbia, and possessed the full confidence and esteem of all who knew him."

"Nathaniel C. Hunter, died April 28, 1812, aged 48 years."

"In memory of Sarah Ann Hunter, widow of J. C. H. who died September 28th, 1815, aged 71 years."

There are two stones to children. Constant Chapman's will is authority for the burial of Jonathan Chapman and other relatives in the same enclosure. She directed that she be buried there. The Fairfax order book of 1789 designates Summer Hill, as "George Chapman's home plantation". As she died two years later, it is probable she was buried there, but no stone marks her grave.

"Chapman's Quarter", devised by Simon Pearson to his daughter Constantia, was conveyed by her toward the end of her life, to her son George and passed by his will to his wife, Amelia. By two deeds made in 1817 and 1819 it passed to her son, Dr. Nathaniel Chapman of Philadelphia. In 1833 he transferred to John Biddle Chapman also of Philadelphia (Arlington D. B., V 2 page 1). As Dr. Chapman married into the Biddle family, the grantee was probably his son. John Biddle Chapman died about 1850 and the tract containing 431 acres was sold in a chancery proceeding to Bushrod W. Hunter (Arlington D.B., M-3 p 395). He was a great grandson of Constant Chapman. He divided it into twenty acre lots and sold most of them. What remained passed to his daughter Sally B. Hunter and was still owned by her in the year 1900. The tract is east of the Glebe Road. The Lee Boulevard runs through the center of it and the Columbia Gardens Cemetery occupies some thirty acres of it.

Chapman's Mill is on Broad Run in the gap of the Bull Run Mountains. The present mill is the successor of an earlier one, whose ruined stone walls still stand. A tablet high up on the wall of the existing mill bears the inscription,

"From Jonathan Chapman
Nathaniel Chapman

87

> Pearson Chapman
> John Chapman
> George Chapman
> To   John Chapman,
> rebuilt 1858"

The John and George Chapman whose names follow that of Pearson were his sons. John is said to have willed the mill to his brother George. The last John was presumably the son of this George Chapman.

A little below the mill are the broken walls of an old Chapman house and behind it is a buying plot containing a small obelisk to "George Chapman by his wife". A large grave stone beside it bears the inscription, "To the memory of our dear mother, Susan Pearson, consort of George Chapman born 1780 died 1856".

THE BALL PATENTS

The Glencarlyn plateau embraced in John and Moses Ball's patents was probably first traversed by white men about 1680. The Indian war of 1676 led to an act of the Provincial Assembly authorizing the governor of the colony to appoint a lieutenant for each frontier county, who was required to raise eleven men from the neighborhood with horses and arms. It was the business of such detachments to scour the woods above the settlements for hostile Indians. The journal kept by one of the Potomac rangers for 1692 has been preserved, and tells of ranging the country from Accotink to Sugarland Run. These men must have passed through Glencarlyn, or very near it, on some of their expeditions.

The grants along Four Mile Run, which began with the Howsing patent of 1669 have been enumerated in previous papers. By 1735 all land bordering the run up to its source at Falls Church had passed to private owners, except the Glencarlyn tract. A sprinkling of settlers was spread over the neighborhood. Cabins had been built and clearings made in the forest. For some reason this tract was the last to be taken up. It remained without an owner other than Lord Fairfax until 1742 when John Ball got a grant for it. As the patents heretofore mentioned were drawn on the same model, the Ball patent will serve to show the form of grant in which all titles in this part of Virginia originate.

John Ball's Deed for 166 acres of land, Fairfax County.

The Right Honorable Thomas Lord Fairfax, Baron of Cameron in that part of Great Britain called Scotland, Proprietor of the Northern Neck of Virginia,—To all to whom this present writing shall come sends Greetings:—

Know ye that for good causes for and in consideration of the Composition for my use paid, And for the annual rent hereafter reserved, I have given, granted & confirmed, And by these presents for me and my heirs & assigns, Do give grant & confirm unto John Ball of the County of Fairfax, One certain tract of waste Land in sd County Bounded according to a survey thereof made by Mr. George Byrn as followeth, Beginning at a white oak in the fork of four mile run called the long branch & running No 88° Wt three hundred thirty eight poles to the Line of Capt. Pearson, then with the line of Pearson No 34° Et One hundred Eighty-eight poles to a Gum on the So Wt side of the run corner to Pearsons red oak & chestnut Land, then down the run & binding therewith So 54° Et Two hundred & ninety poles to the beginning, Containing One hundred Sixty six Acres, Together with all rights members & appurtenances thereunto belonging, Royal mines Excepted, And a full third part of all Lead, Copper, Tinn, Coals, Iron mines & Iron ore, that shall be found thereon; To have & to hold the sd hundred & sixty six Acres of Land, Together with all rights profits & benefits to the same belonging, or in any wise appertaining, Except before Excepted, To him the sd John Ball his heirs & Assigns forever; He the sd John Ball his heirs & assigns therefore Yielding & Paying unto me my heirs & assigns or to my certain Attorney or Attorneys, Agent or Agents, or to certain Attorney or Attorneys of my heirs & assigns, Proprietors of the sd northern neck yearly &c. every year on the feast day of St. Michael the Archangel the fee rent of one Shilling sterling money for every fifty acres of Land hereby granted & so proportionably for a greater or lesser quantity. Provided, That if the sd John Ball, his heirs & assigns shall not pay the before reserved annual rent so that the same or any part thereof shall be behind or unpaid by the space of two whole years after the same shall come due if lawfully demanded. That then it shall & may be lawful for me my heirs or assigns Proprietors as aforesaid my or their certain Attorney or Attorneys, Agent or Agents into the above granted premises to Reenter & hold the same so as if this

90

grant had never passed. Given at my office in the County of Fairfax within my sd Proprietary under my Seal. Witness my Agent & Attorney fully authorized thereto. Dated the fifteenth day of January in the Sixteenth year of the Reign of our Sovereign Lord George the Second, by the grace of God of great Brittain, France & Ireland King Defender of the Faith &c. Anni One thousand seven hundred & forty two.

W. Fairfax.

Recorded in Northern Neck Land Book "F", page 57.

W. Fairfax was William Fairfax of Belvoir, cousin and then agent for Lord Fairfax, who was in England when the patent was issued. The Act forming Fairfax County was signed by the Governor on June 19th, 1742, but had passed the House of Burgesses in the preceding year, and William Fairfax, who was then a Burgess for Prince William County, was anticipating its passage when he located the land in Fairfax County.

The first course of the patent runs almost due west from its starting point at the junction of Long Branch with Four Mile Run in a straight line for a mile, along the south boundary of the subdivision of Glencarlyn and continues in the middle of the road from Reynold's corner to the turn at Hummers. The second course runs northeasterly to Four Mile Run across the field formerly belonging to Torreyson. A line of trees marks its location. Mrs. Charles H. Seaton's westerly line is the only part of this second course which is still a dividing line between different owners.

It is certain John Ball made his home on the tract soon after he got his patent. He and his family did not long remain the sole occupants of the Glencarlyn tract. After he took out his patent, there remained a parcel of ninety-one acres adjoining on the south, belonging to the Proprietor, surrounded on all sides by land which had passed to private ownership. This was a narrow strip between John Ball on the north, Simon Pearson on the south, Stephen Gray on the east and Thomas Pearson on the west. On May 26th,

1748, Lord Fairfax granted this strip to Moses Ball,[1] describing it as a tract on the branches of Four Mile Run, beginning at a white oak standing in the fork of a branch of Four Mile Run and extending thence west along the line of John Ball 343 poles to a hickory; thence south twenty-seven degrees west 44 poles to a red oak a corner of Captain Pearson; thence running east and binding with John Alexander's line 362 poles; thence south along said Alexander's line 70 poles to a white oak a corner of Stephen Gray; thence north twenty-four degrees east binding with Stephen Gray's line 80 poles to a white oak on the south side of Four Mile Run; thence up meanders of the run north sixty-three degrees west 40 poles to the beginning, containing ninety-one acres. The Alexander lines were lines of the Simon Pearson patent. He had willed it to his daughter Susanna who had married John Alexander. Guy Broadwater was recited to have made the survey. The tract was a mile long with a breadth varying from four hundred to six hundred feet. Its peculiar shape is explained by the fact that it was a vacancy left over from the prior grants. Though he may have cultivated it earlier, Moses Ball did not make his residence there until 1755. The Sarah Anderson house is at the east end, and the Hummer house at the west end of the patent.

Who were John and Moses Ball and where did they live before getting their grants? John Ball's patent recites him as resident in Fairfax in 1742, and Moses Ball's patent locates him in Fairfax in 1748. There is evidence that Moses Ball lived in Hunting Creek Valley before he moved to Four Mile Run. John Ball probably lived in that neighborhood but the evidence is inferential. The names of both appear on the list of voters at the election of Burgesses for Prince William County in 1741 and Prince William then included Fairfax.[2] Both voted at the Fairfax election of Burgesses in 1744,[2] and on each occasion they voted for Colonel John Colville, whose house was on the south side of Great

---

[1] N.N., F – 288.

[2] Boogher's Gleanings in Virginia History.

Hunting Creek. As neither John nor Moses Ball had their patents in 1741, their voting indicates that both of them owned land acquired by descent or devise. The ownership of twenty-five acres was required by law to vote at elections.

The Ball family Bible gives 1717 as the date of Moses Ball's birth. He has descendants in southwestern Virginia who are seeking information about his ancestors. Recently this notice was posted in the Glencarlyn post office: "Wanted: the name of the father of Moses Ball, who lived on Four Mile Run, and who died in 1792, and is buried at or near Clarendon in the Ball burying ground". This interested the wife of the writer of this article, and after considerable search, she answered the question. There was an earlier John Ball, who in 1695 patented two hundred twenty-one acres on the north branches of Little Hunting Creek.[2] This John Ball also bought from Robert Brent executor of Nicholas Brent three hundred forty three acres situate on the north side of Hunting Creek beginning a "little below the wading place" and extending above it, by deeds of lease and release dated July 11 and 12 in 1715. (see recital in first Fairfax Survey Book page 25). It was part of a tract patented by George Brent of "Woodstock" which had passed under his will to his son Nicholas. John Ball removed to the bank of Hunting Creek shortly after acquiring this tract. This John Ball left a will proved in County Court of Stafford, as shown by the index. The book in which it was recorded (Liber K) is missing, but it covers the period of 1721 to 1730. He was the father of Moses Ball. The latter testified in two suits over the western boundary line of the Howsing patent. His depositions are preserved as a part of the record in the suit of Alexander vs Birch. He stated that he was the son of John Ball; that he lived from his birth to 1741 on the bank of Hunting Creek about a half mile above the ford or crossing place,

---

[2] N. N., Land Grants 2–188. It was located a mile west of the Groveton School and near the old Collard House, recently bought by Senator La Follette.

and that from then to 1755 he lived on the Potomac River eight or nine miles from the ford, and since had lived about five or six miles from the ford (which is its distance from his patent at Glencarlyn); that he had a brother James born in 1698, and another brother John, born in 1714. [4] James was probably his half brother.

The Register of Overwharton Parish (which then included Prince William and Fairfax Counties as well as the part of Stafford County around Aquia and Potomac Churches) still exists for the years 1730 to 1753 and shows the baptisms, deaths and marriages of some of this John Ball's children and grandchildren during the last years of his life. Neither John or Moses Ball appear on the Register as they were born before 1730. These entries suggest that John Ball of Stafford was married twice; that by his first marriage he had sons, James, William (who married Winifred Williams) and Caleb; and that by his second marriage had sons, George, John Jr., and Moses. John Ball of Glencarlyn named one of his daughters Winifred. It is probable then that he was the son of the William Ball who married Winifred Williams.

No relationship has yet been traced between this Ball family and the descendants of Colonel William Ball of Millenbeck, great grandfather of George Washington. One of the baptisms recorded in the Overwharton register is that

---

[4] This John Ball was probably the millwright whom Washington employed to rebuild his mill on Dogue run in 1770. The restoration of the mill bears an inscription that it was built in 1760. The diaries show the mill was badly damaged by a freshet in that year and that a new mill was under consideration, but apparently the old mill was then repaired, as after the repairs were completed Washington made an entry that "all her works were decayed and out of order" (April 8, 1760). The entries from December, 1769, to July 1770, show the mill was completely rebuilt under the superintendence of John Ball. The diaries show he was then living at Cameron, probably on part of the Brent patent, bought by his father from the executor of Nicholas Brent.

of Lydia Peck Ball in 1749. She was a child of John Ball Jr. and Margaret Williams Ball his wife. There was a Ball family which migrated from England to Connecticut in the seventeenth century; a branch of it removed to East Jersey and took a prominent part in the founding of Newark. There were Moses Balls in that family, and a Lydia Ball of New Jersey married Joseph Peck. The available data seem then to indicate that John and Moses Ball of Glencarlyn and the earlier John Ball of Stafford descend from the New Jersey Balls; and that John Ball of Stafford came from New Jersey to Virginia before 1700. However that may be, it is certain that this Ball family was one of the pioneer families of Fair fax County and had located in the territory between Great and Little Hunting Creeks before the end of the seventeenth century.

Frank L. Ball, former state senator, and E. Wade Ball, former treasurer of Arlington County, are descendants of Moses Ball through his son Ensign John Ball.

It was John Ball and Moses Ball who cleared the forest, grubbed the stumps, ploughed the virgin soil, raised the first crops of tobacco, corn and wheat, planted the first orchards, built the first fences, and somewhere on our plateau reared the first dwellings, with their barns and outbuildings. John Ball may have built the still standing part of the old Carlin House. The great hand-hewn rafter beams testify to its age. The present owner, was told that it was built in 1759, but his informant did not give the source of his information. As to the location of Moses Ball's house, the evidence is that it stood just south of the barn of Mr. Oliver H. King. An old resident states that an old pear tree was there when she first remembers, and that it was common knowledge a house had once stood there. Immediately south is a spring whose copious flow withstood the drought of 1930. The spot was near the center of Moses Ball's elongated farm, and also near John Ball's house.

Though the Ball patents were issued later than those for the adjoining land, there is reason to believe they were cleared and farmed first. The Colville tract on the north, the Gray-Mercer tract on the east, the Pearson-Alexander tract on the south all belonged to non-resident owners. The tract to the west, comprising the land between Munson Hill and Four Mile Run, though patented by Thomas Pearson in 1708, was never a Pearson residence. The Prince William records show that his grandson also named Thomas made two leases for separate parts of it, in 1740 and 1741. This indicates that its clearing and cultivation began about the same time as that of the Glencarlyn neighborhood. A visitor to the Ball cabins in 1760 would have seen cleared land and woodland in substantially the same proportions and the same places as they exist today, but he would have found the Baileys Cross-Roads, the Bon Air and the Veitch localities still deep in the forest.

OLD MILLS

The evidence points to the existence of two early mills, one on Moses Ball's land, and the other on John Ball's. The approximate location of Moses Ball's mill is fixed by an entry in Washington's Diary. In 1774 Washington bought a tract fronting on Four Mile Run from George and James Mercer. It was the land included in the patents of Stephen Gray and Gabriel Adams. Moses Ball's land had a frontage on Four Mile Run, extending from the mouth of Long Branch southeasterly 40 poles or six hundred sixty feet, according to his patent. Stephen Gray's patent adjoined Moses Ball on the east. Washington was looking for the westerly line of Gray's patent. The entry is: "Friday April 22nd 1785; took an early breakfast at Abingdon and accompanied by Dr. Stewart, and Lund Washington, and having sent for Mr. Moses Ball (who attended) I went to a corner of the above land, within about three poles of the run (Four Mile Run), a white oak eighteen inches in diameter, on the side of a hill, about one hundred fifty yards below the ruins of an old mill.[5] On

---

[5] Diaries Vol. 2 p. 366.

the hill side about one hundred forty yards westerly from the spot where Washington commenced his survey, there is still an excavation in the ground and what seems to be the remains of an old mill race can yet be traced. The race was fed by Long Branch and not by Four Mile Run. As Moses Ball's patent was not forty years old when Washington made his survey, the mill must have had a brief existence.

There is also a tradition in our community of another mill further up Four Mile Run above the mouth of Long Branch on John Ball's tract and on the border of the Glencarlyn Park. This could not have been the mill Washington referred to as it is half a mile west of his land. There is record evidence of its existence.

Colonel John Colville owned the Lubber Run tract fronting on Four Mile Run across from John Ball's land. In 1755 he had a survey made of it, a copy of which is recorded in the oldest Fairfax County Book of Surveys, (Surveys 1748-1767). Incidentally, the survey shows the outline of John Ball's tract on the south side of the run and on Ball's land about opposite the mouth of Lubber Run is shown a small square with the words "Mill House". An inspection of the traditional location shows a dozen or more drills in the rocks where the dam is supposed to have stood. Below the dam the evidence of an outlet race seems plain. Above the dam, the railroad embankment has destroyed all trace of the race. John Ball's will refers to his "mill stock" and the inventory of his estate, preserved at Fairfax Court House, enumerates "a broken pair of millstones" and "a pair of new millstones, frog and spindle".

There were at least two more colonial mills on Four Mile Run. The Fairfax County order book shows that in February 1754 Colonel John Colville was given permission to erect a water grist mill. It was built on Lubber Run a short distance above its confluence with Four Mile Run. Traces of its mill race remain. Further down the Run below Cowden was the mill originally known as Chubb's. It is first mentioned in a patent of 1719 and was operating

in 1790 as Adams' Mill.[6]   A civil war map of 1861 shows it
as Roach's Mill.

Shortly before Washington was appointed to command
the Army at Cambridge, he was solicited by a Jacob Gooding of "Four Mile Run" to lease him part of the land bought
of James and George Mercer, and to finance the building of
"a convenient mill both for merchant and country work and
perhaps a saw mill, and if I think country manufactured
cloth is likely to be encouraged, will also build a good fulling
mill".[7]   The Revolutionary War stopped the project, if
Washington ever considered it.

A walk through the woods down Holmes Run from the
crossing of the Columbia Turnpike to the Little River Turnpike reveals the sites of several abandoned mills overgrown
by thickets.   The number of mill sites in this limited area
is surprising.   Possibly Moses and John Balls' mills were
intended primarily to grind their own corn and wheat, but
Chubb's mill, Colville's mill and Gooding's projected mill
are reminiscent of a change then taking place in the agriculture of Northern Virginia.   By the middle of the eighteenth century, Fairfax County was substituting wheat for
tobacco as its chief export crop.[8]

THE FIRST ROAD TO GLENCARLYN

As soon as John and Moses Ball took possession of
their lands, the question of an outlet road became important.   The roads of Fairfax were then few and little more
than trails.   Neither of the Ball patents bordered on a
road.   The nearest road was the trail leading from Alexandria past Falls Church, and the first court house of the
county at Freedom Hill, and thence over the Blue Ridge by
Vestal's Gap.   It was the precursor of the present Alexan-

[6] Christopher Colles Road Map of U.S. 1790.
[7] Letters to Washington – Murray – V – 105.
[8] Landmarks of Old Prince William p. 401.

dria and Leesburg Turnpike. There is some reason to believe that the section of this road from Bailey's Cross-Roads to Falls Church then ran near the existing road between these points. Moses Ball's tract was nearer this road than John Ball's. At its southwest corner it was about a quarter of a mile from the spot on the Alexandria and Leesburg Road where Head's blacksmith shop stood. The land between was in Thomas Pearson's patent, which included Munson Hill. Whether by agreement with the owner of that land, or otherwise, the Balls laid off a road leading from the present Head's corner through the Pearson tract until it reached Moses Ball's corner on the rise south of Long Branch; thence along Moses Ball's west line across the branch and up the hill to Hummer's corner and the southwest corner of John Ball; thence easterly between Moses and John Ball as far as the present Backus house. When the mills on Four Mile Run were built, the road was necessarily extended to connect with them. It passed between the two Ball houses. The interesting fact about this first road is that from Head's corner to Reynold's corner, the road is still in use and follows its course as originally laid off, while east of Reynold's corner it is wholly disused and has been disused for a century. The tradition of the road still persists, and at spots it can still be identified by slight depressions and by a line of cedar trees.

After the establishment of these mills, a second road was opened through the woods leading east across Four Mile Pun to what is now the Glebe Road, as there is a reference to "John Ball's mill path" in one of the depositions in the suit of Alexander vs Birch and another as late as 1815. [9]

The first road from Rosslyn, then Awbrey's Ferry, to the Falls Church via Upton Hill, (the precursor of Wilson Boulevard), is also an old road going back beyond the middle of the eighteenth century. Early deeds call it Awbrey's Road [10], but the connection from Reynold's corner to

---

[9] Arlington D.B., Z–83.
[10] Arlington D.B., E2–273.

Ballston was not made until many years later. The earliest reference I have found to it is a deed made in 1848, though it was doubtless in existence before then.

THE ALEXANDRIA AND LEESBURG ROAD

The outlet road gave the Balls a route to the Potomac River and to the road leading to Hunting Creek and thence south through Dumfries. This road has borne several different names. At this time, it was generally called the court house road because it passed near the first court house of Fairfax County at Freedom Hill, near Tysons. It is somewhat surprising to learn that this first court house was established so far inland. The reason was that Fairfax County included Loudoun until 1758. When Loudoun became a separate county, the court house was moved to Alexandria, but the road continued to be called "the road leading to the old court house". Later it was styled the "middle turnpike" because it lay between the Little River Turnpike and the Georgetown and Leesburg Road over Chain Bridge; and still later, (and at present), it bore the name of the Alexandria and Leesburg Road. The existing road from Falls Church to Alexandria is fairly straight, but the old road of 1750 reached its destination by many windings. It ran southeasterly through or near the present Baileys Cross Roads; then it followed the course of the present Seminary Road half way to the Theological Seminary. Here it forked. When Washington was surveying his land many years later, the "widow Tucker" had a house and plantation there. The left fork going toward Alexandria is now all but obliterated and impassible by automobile, though still shown as a road on some modern maps. It passed close to the Civil War earthwork of Fort Ward, thence by the Casenave Lee land and came into the present Alexandria and Leesburg Road north of the Episcopal High School where the road north from the Seminary also intersects; thence it went on through Braddock Heights and reached the north end of Alexandria. The other fork followed the existing Seminary Road eastward through William Henry Terrett's patent and eventually crossed Hunting Creek at "the wading place" where the present "telegraph road" crosses, joining the then existing back road passing the site of the future Pohick Church and the Occoquan. The present Alexandria and Leesburg Road must have been opened before 1826 as the will of William Henry Terrett made in that year devised land on the "south side of the old Leesburg Road".[11]

THE MONUMENT

At the junction of Four Mile Run and Long Branch stands the monument erected by the Glencarlyn Citizens Association bearing this inscription; "On this spot stood an oak tree bearing a survey mark made by George Washington, which became a monumental survey mark named in many deeds".

The spot deserves a marker and we may well be grateful to the citizens Association for placing it there. Three original patents meet in the middle of Four Mile Run at the mouth of Long Branch. North of the run is the Lubber Run Tract patented to Major John Colville on February 4, 1731. The surveyor is recited to be Henry Warner. On the south side of the run this point is the beginning point of John Ball's one hundred sixty-six acre tract and as already stated, the surveyor was George Byrn. The same point is the beginning of Moses Ball's patent, the surveyor being Guy Broadwater. In 1755 John Colville caused another survey to be made of his tract a copy of which is recorded in oldest book of surveys at Fairfax Courthouse. G. W. West was the surveyor and Moses Ball one of the chain carriers. That Washington visited this spot is highly probable. The corner of his tract was some six hundred feet further down

---

[11] Fairfax Wills O-136.

101

the run, and we know from his diaries that he made four different starts on a survey of his land, one of which he did not complete because of an accident to his chain bearer. The only questionable statement in the inscription is that the oak tree standing there bore his survey mark. Washington retained his zest for surveying throughout his life. He never employed another to survey his lands when it was practicable for him to do it himself. His four surveys of his Four Mile Run land were all made when he was upwards of fifty. They were evidently labors of love and the diaries show he took congenial friends along with him. It must have been a treat for Moses Ball to be one of a party with General Washington, Dr. Stuart and Lund Washington. We shall see that he turned the occasion to good account later. But after the French and Indian War, when Washington had become a man of consequence, it is unlikely that he did any surveying for hire. The oak tree "which bore a survey mark made by George Washington" may have been the "white oak eighteen inches in diameter on the side of the run" mentioned in the diary.

JOHN BALL

The records of the Fairfax County Court show that John Ball had his share of litigation. Among other suits, he brought an action of trespass against Daniel French, the builder of Pohick Church, whose home and plantation was at Rose Hill, on the Fairfax Rolling Road south of Cameron Run. In the same year he acquired his Four Mile Run tract, Ball had patented one hundred forty acres between the drains of Dogue Run and Cameron Run.[12] When he attempted to take possession, French disputed his title, so he sued him in trespass, as a way of trying title. The court ordered the jury to view the land, and in 1748 Daniel Jennings, the county surveyor, in the presence of the jury

---

[12] N.N., F-140.

ran the lines of both parties. Ball produced his patent and French produced an earlier patent of 1730 to his father, Daniel French, the elder. The two patents conflicted, and Ball lost his suit and the land. He died in 1766, twenty-four years after he had settled on his Four Mile Run patent. He was probably buried on his land, possibly in the present Carlin Burial lot. His will is of record at Fairfax.[13] It directs that his land, plantation and mill stock be sold, and the money therefrom equally divided among his wife and his five daughters and he appointed his "true and trusty friends William Adams and Moses Ball" his executors. Apparently he left no son. While he calls Moses Ball "his friend", I have set out my reasons for believing that they were distant relations. His wife's name was Elizabeth. Her maiden name is not known. She survived her husband, and when his will was proved, she came into court and elected to take her dower, instead of taking under the will. Accordingly one-third of his land was assigned to her for her life. She was still on the land in 1792, as a deed made by William Carlin in that year mentions the dividing line between Carlin and Elizabeth Ball. From a suit brought some years later it appears that the five daughters of John Ball all married:—Stacy to John Dowdall, Mary to Moses Hardin, Milly to William Thompson; Winifred to John Rollings; and the fifth daughter to James Gray. Moses Ball appears to have been the only acting executor.[14] His

---

[13] Fairfax Will Book B p. 462.

[14] The Fairfax Order Book shows that Moses Ball's administration of John Ball's estate was not satisfactory to the latter's daughters as he was twice summoned to appear at the next court and render an account of the estate. He succeeded, however, in recovering for the estate judgment for one hundred forty pounds against the executors of John Minor, on a bond of the latter. The facts are obscure, but they appear in some way to have involved the suit in trespass by Ball against French, for the plaintiff put in evidence the record of that case to show the eviction of John Ball from the land he claimed, and the forfeiture of the bond of John Minor to John Ball.

inventory of the estate is of record at the court house. It tells something of the contents of the first house built in Glencarlyn. Some of the articles enumerated are: an old smooth bore gun, old foot adze, an old tennant saw, six sheep, two cows, two heifers, two yearlings, one grey mare, two sows and twelve pigs, one pair of spectacles, one woolen wheel, one iron box and heaters, a parcel of old books, one pair of old fire tongs, old fiddle, one old oval table, one old looking glass, five yards of woolen cloth, two old linnen wheels, three beds, two old bed hides, half dozen best plates, half dozen delph plates, four earthen ditto, eleven knives, twelve forks, four earthen pans, parcel of earthenware, one still, tub and worm, three old axes, two bells, one saddle and bridle, plough, seven casks, pack of cards, one flax bake, four bee hives, three syder troughs, grindstone, broken pair of millstones, pair of new millstones, frog and spindle, ten geese, one old hat, jacket and britches.

The final account of Moses Ball acting executor gives the names of many persons in the locality with whom John Ball had business and to whom he owed money, or who owed money to him. Among them were: Sampson Darrell, who was sheriff of Fairfax County in 1767 and lived at Darrell's Hill, a mile south of Alexandria; Reverend James Muir, pastor of the Presbyterian Congregation in Alexandria; Captain John Dalton, merchant at Alexandria; William Ellzey, the lawyer who advised the executor; Robert Harrison of Alexandria; John Bowling, who lived somewhere in the neighborhood, as his tract is named as a boundary in other deeds of land in the vicinity of Bailey's Cross-Roads; William Adams, | whom John Ball named as one of his executors; and who owned and operated a mill on Holmes Run where the Columbia Turnpike crosses; Captain John Minor, a vestryman of Truro Parish (1744–1748).[15]

---

[15] As already stated John Ball's executor sued John Minor's executor. Minor lived on the south side of Great Hunting Creek where the Telegraph Road crosses. A note to Washington's Diaries (which seems to be based on information gathered from Land Marks of Old

The quarter of a century that John Ball spent here was a period of rapid increase in population and well being in the neighborhood. All danger from Indians had vanished. The tobacco warehouse landing above Hunting Creek had been erected into the town of Alexandria by an Act of the Assembly passed in 1749, and was rapidly growing into a small city. Colchester on the Occoquan was chartered as a town in 1753. The mills and warehouse at Saw Pit Landing became Georgetown in 1754, while further away Winchester was growing into a place of importance. Leesburg had become a court house hamlet. The great estates in the lower end of the county, Gunston, Belvoir and Mount Vernon were seats of wealth and hospitality. Elsewhere in eastern Fairfax were the substantial homes and plantations of the McCartys of Cedar Grove, the Bronaghs of Newtown, the Chichesters of Newington, the Frenches of Rose Hill, the Washingtons of Hayfield, the Wests of West Grove, the Johnsons of Belvale, the Tripletts of Round Hill, the Colvilles of Cleesh, the Alexanders of Abingdon, the Cockburns of Springfield, the Wageners on the Occoquan, the Cliftons of Clifton's Ferry, later called Wellington,

---

Prince William), states that "In 1746 John Colville and John Minor sought to establish a town at the head of Hunting Creek, in rivalry to the 'Belhaven' which was then growing up about the Hunting Creek warehouse on the Potomac. Bidding for the support of Lord Fairfax, they gave this proposed town the name of Cameron. Although their plans were urged upon the Assembly in 1749, when the petition to establish Alexandria was under consideration, they failed. Though there never was anything on the site, but the ordinary, or tavern, marked on the Jefferson and Fry map of 1755, the name persisted because it marked the junction of all roads leading into Alexandria. Races and musters of the militia were held there, and the Truro Vestry made it the point of departure of processionings. At the end of the century the 'Cameron Mills' perpetuated the tradition, and the waters which actuated those mills are still marked 'Cameron Run' on the modern map."

Diaries Vol. 1 p. 283.

Catesby Cooke on the Occoquan; Edward Washington of Belmont, the Emersons on the hills southwest from Alexandria.

In 1772 Moses Ball, as executor of John Ball, conveyed, or attempted to convey, the John Ball farm to William Carlin, and put him in possession. I shall have more to say of that transaction presently.

WILLIAM CARLIN

William Carlin was born at Peasley Bridge in Yorkshire, England, in 1732. He had two brothers and a sister, but was the only member of his family to migrate to America.[16] He was in Alexandria before 1770, and purchased a lot there.[17] His descendants have preserved the tradition that he was "tailor to George Washington". I find in Washington's Diaries this entry:

"February 4, 1770 At home all day. Carlin, the Taylor, came here (Mt. Vernon) and stayed all night".[18] A note by the editor states that this was William Carlin of Alexandria. Additional evidence of the identity of William Carlin, the tailor, of Alexandria, with William Carlin who purchased John Ball's farm is that a tailor's goose, an heirloom of the Carlin family, was given by the late William H. F. Carlin to the late Mr. Plant of our village. The Diaries show that there was another William Carlin (Washington spells his name Carlain) in Fairfax County in the eighteenth century, but his home was on the old Braddock Road near Centerville, where he furnished lodging and meals to travellers. Washington occasionally put up at his house,[19] but nothing suggests that he was related to Wilam Carlin, the Yorkshire emigrant.

---

[16] Information by Mr. Lewis Carlin of Washington City.
[17] M – 100 Fairfax Land Records.
[18] Diaries 1–264.
[19] Diaries 1–336.

The deed book containing the record of the deed from Moses Ball, executor, to William Carlin in the year 1772 was destroyed during the Civil War. Its existence is attested by recitals in a later deed, from which it appears that the purchase price was one hundred pounds. Carlin took possession under color of this deed. The deed, however, was defective and gave Carlin only an equitable title. John Ball's will had directed the sale of his land and appointed William Adams and Moses Ball, executors. The deed of one of them did not pass a good title. The defect was discovered thirteen years later, and in 1785 Moses Ball and William Adams, executors, made a confirmatory deed, the record of which is in a surviving deed book [20] reciting the error of the prior deed, and conveying the one hundred sixty-six acres by the metes and bounds of the original patent. Although this deed does not mention it, one-third of the one hundred sixty-six acres was in the possession of Elizabeth Ball, as her dower interest. Possession could not be delivered until her death. But Carlin was not through with his troubles. The order book of Fairfax County shows that on May 21, 1788 an ejectment suit brought by the five daughters of John Ball and their husbands against William Carlin, came on for trial before a jury. The county courts in Virginia at that time were not presided over by a single lawyer-judge, but by a court made up of elected justices who were not usually lawyers, but gentlemen landowners. The record shows the justices who sat at the hearing were David Stuart, Charles Alexander, William Herbert and Roger West. They were all men of local consequence in their day. Dr. David Stuart had married the widow of John Parke Custis and was one of Washington's most valued friends. He was then living at Abingdon on the Potomac above the mouth of Four Mile Run. Charles Alexander (1737–1806) was the owner of a large tract near Alexandria, part of the Howsing patent, on which he lived. He was a son of John Alexander and Susanna Pearson his wife and was the plain-

---

[20] Fairfax D.B. Liber P – 440.

tiff in Alexander vs Birch. William Herbert had married the daughter of John Carlyle. He was Mayor of Alexandria and later a banker there. Roger West was the son of Col. John West and Margaret Pearson West. He was a delegate to the Virginia Legislature in 1788 and married the daughter of James Craik, Washington's physician. The jury returned a directed verdict in favor of Carlin. A memorandum on the order book shows the point at issue. John Ball had directed his land to be sold, but he had not specifically directed his executors to make the sale. The plaintiffs contended that the sale should have been made by a trustee appointed by the court. The law has long been settled that in such a case the executor has an implied power of sale.

If Moses Ball turned over the proceeds of sale to John Ball's daughters as he undoubtedly did, the suit was shoddy business. John Ball's daughters were seeking to take advantage of their disability as married women. An appeal was noted but nothing came of it, as Carlin remained in possession. He seems to have prospered, as he bought three more tracts. The first of these was one hundred sixty-five acres on the north side of Four Mile Run across from his original tract. This was part of Colonel John Colville's Lubber Run tract.[21] The deed to Carlin was made by the Honorable Charles Earl of Tankerville and the Honorable Henry A. Ashton, devisees of the late Earl of

[21] Fairfax D.B., U–12. Though now wholly forgotten except by the student of local history, Colonel John Colville played a considerable part in the early history of northern Virginia, ranking with William Fairfax and Lawrence Washington. He was vestryman of Truro Parish from 1734 to 1748; a burgess from 1744 to 1748, Lawrence Washington was his colleague. A note by the editor of Washington's Diaries (Vol. 1 p. 214) states: "John Colville was trading in the Potomac in his own ship in 1730, and soon thereafter seated himself on land he called Clish on the lower side of Great Hunting Creek. He served as Justice and Burgess, and accumulated large bodies of land, chiefly in the Catoctin neighborhood before he died in 1756, and left

Tankerville who had acquired title by the will of John Colville. This one hundred sixty-five acres included the Mary A. Carlin land (now Lane) the Paullin and Alexander parcels and a considerable part of the Henderson estate. It was bounded on the west by the present Bon Air subdivision and extended along the road to Ballston as far as the hill above Lubber Run. The next parcel Carlin bought contained about three acres acquired from Thomas Green Hardin, a nephew of Moses Ball, also on the north bank of Four Mile Run.[22] By another deed executed in 1794 he acquired from Andrew Wales the Gladding patent, calling for one hundred nineteen acres, but actually containing one hundred two acres.[23] This lay on both sides of the present Columbia Turnpike and included the Kline and Kaldenback farms northeast of the road connecting Glencarlyn

---

the bulk of his estate to the Earl of Tankerville. Meanwhile his brother Thomas had emigrated to Cecil County, Maryland, but on John's death, removed to Clish to administer on John's estate." Bryan Fairfax subsequently purchased four hundred acres of the Clish estate on which he built Mt. Eagle. Colvin Run is supposed to have been named after John Colville. Among his numerous patents was one for 5568 acres on both sides of Difficult Run, which he sold to William Fairfax in 1740. (Prince William D. B. Liber E folio 203 and 207, lease and release). These refer to the ford over Difficult Run where a bridge formerly stood and show that the ford had been bridged before 1740, at or near the present bridge. It shows how rapidly Fairfax County was being settled that a bridge should have been built there so early.

Although a vestryman, Colville made no bones of setting out in his will (Fairfax Will Book B.97) that he had a natural daughter by Mary Foster "who came into the country on my ship and when free continued with me for several years". The daughter Catherine married John West, Jr. Colville made provisions in his will for both the mother and daughter. He gave the name of his home as "Cleesh" (not Clish) and left it to his brother Thomas for life.

[22] Fairfax D.B. Liber Y fol. 220.
[23] Fairfax D.B. Liber Y fol. 193.

with the turnpike. For the Lubber Run tract he paid the high price of $15.00 an acre, giving a purchase money mortgage. It was all woodland then and is mostly woodland still. These purchases brought his holdings up to near four hundred fifty acres. Carlin had one more suit over the Ball patent, against John Ball's widow, Elizabeth for waste. Presumably, she was cutting standing timber.

In 1792 he granted Edward Skidmore and Lydia his wife a life estate in land at the southwest corner of the tract he had bought from John Ball's executors.[24] It adjoined the land of Moses Ball and the dower land of Elizabeth Ball. The Skidmore and Carlin families were closely connected. One of Carlin's sons, James Harvey Carlin, married Litia Skidmore. She was probably the daughter of the Edward and Lydia Skidmore mentioned above, and the name Litia is likely a variation of Lydia. A grandson of William Carlin, William H. F. Carlin married Margaret Skidmore.

William Carlin, the immigrant, was married twice. His first wife was a Miss Payne. Her christian name is unknown. There were several families of that name in Fairfax in the eighteenth century, so it is probable his first marriage took place after he reached Virginia. His second wife was Elizabeth Hall who survived him. He left issue by both marriages.

The Fairfax County order book of 1789 (September Court) contains a list of the tithables who were ordered to work on the county roads. It gives a glimpse of the farms along the Alexandria and Leesburg Road in our vicinity.

"On the road from the white oak at widow Tucker's (a mile and a half east of Baileys Cross Roads) to Falls Church; tithables; James Daniel, John Dowdall, Hay Harding, James Ball, William Donaldson, Andrew Donaldson, William Piper, Thomas Taylor, Thomas Donaldson, William Carlin, Moses Ball, Charles Little's quarter, William Adams, William Bladen, William Merriday, Vincent Taylor, Edward Skidmore, John Thomas, Simon Pearson,

---

[24] Fairfax D. B. Liber U fol. 163.

John Pearson, Whitings Ch. Quarter, John Adams, John Darne, Robert Powell, Joseph Wren, Thomas Gafford's place, James Wren's quarters, George and Mrs. Miner, Ann Bowling, William Thomas, Moses Hardin, Mary Frizzle, Joseph Thompson, John Mills, William Crump, Jr., Joseph Powell's plantations, Caleb Bladen, Henry Hussey, Benjamin Dulany's two quarters, Jonathan Ward, Thomas Pearson, George Thrift, Charles Charters, James Robertson, Samuel Macatee."

"Quarters" signified that the owner did not live on the farm, but worked it through tenants or slaves. Thus, Colonel Charles Little lived at Cleesh, the former seat of Colonel John Colville south of Great Hunting Creek, but owned a plantation on the Falls Church Road. Whiting's Quarter belonged to Carlyle Fairfax Whiting, the grandson of John Carlyle.

James Ball was probably one of the sons of Moses Ball as he had a son of that name who the Virginia Census of 1785 shows lived in a house in this section inhabited by five persons.

CESSION TO THE UNITED STATES

In 1789 the Legislature of Virginia passed an Act ceding to the United States a tract not to exceed ten miles square located in Virginia but retaining jurisdiction until it should be accepted by Congress and a local government provided. Maryland did the same. In 1790 Congress accepted the cession and directed that the president should locate the site. Subsequently the Territory, or District of Columbia was laid off by federal surveyors, and a stone marker placed at each mile. The line ran through the farms of Moses Ball and William Carlin. The seventh marker, which still stands, was placed in Carlin's (later Torreyson's) field. Both the Ball and Carlin houses were in the ceded territory but a part of Carlin's land and a half of Moses Ball's land remained in Fairfax County. It was not

111

until 1800 that Congress assumed jurisdiction. The part of the District lying south of the Potomac River was incorporated in Alexandria County, with its courthouse in the City of Alexandria. It contained about thirty-four square miles.

In 1846 Alexandria County was retroceded to Virginia after a vote of the inhabitants authorized by an Act of Congress. Alexandria City polled a heavy majority for reunion with Virginia. Outside the City the majority voted to remain in the District of Columbia. In 1790 the population of Alexandria County outside the City of Alexandria, was nine hundred seventy-eight persons. In 1840 it was fifteen hundred eight persons.

MOSES BALL'S LAST YEARS

Money troubles clouded Moses Ball's ending years. Washington's Diaries tell part of the story:

"May 16th, 1786. When I returned home, I found Moses Ball and his son John and William Carlin here. The first having his effects under execution, wanted to borrow money to redeem them, lent him ten pounds for the purpose." [25]

Moses may have had a particular reason for bringing his son with him. John Ball had been an ensign in a Virginia regiment during the Revolution. This was one of Washington's many generous loans made to relieve distress. Moses Ball had no claim on him. The only connection between the two was that their lands adjoined.

In 1789 he was obliged to mortgage his farm to William Wilson. [26] Farm mortgages were rare in the eighteenth century.

A census of Fairfax County taken in 1785 contains an entry; "Moses Ball, five in family, one dwelling, two other

---

[25] Diaries 3–61.
[26] Fairfax D.B. Liber 5 folio 10.

buildings". Some of his sons had married and set up establishments of their own. The same census lists Moses Ball, Jr., George Ball and James Ball who were sons of the elder Moses, as independent house holders.

Moses Ball died in 1792. His will made in 1786 is recorded among the Fairfax Wills. [27] He gave to his son John the east twenty-five acres of his farm, beginning at a white oak, corner of General Washington, being all his tract lying east of Long Branch. John never bothered himself to claim it. The balance of his farm, he gave to his wife Ann for her life, and after her death, to his surviving children.

The third paragraph of the will is: "I desire my executors, as soon as possible, to pay his Excellency General Washington the sum of ten pounds with interest, a sum I borrowed from him and William Carlin, security, for which to secure Mr. Carlin, I have given him an Instrument of Writing mentioning two Cows and Yearlings, tho only intending said sum of ten pounds to be made out of the aforesaid cattle in case he (Mr. Carlin) should be obliged to pay General Washington".

The will was made immediately after Washington's loan which may well have been repaid before Ball's death six years later.

If the introductory clause of the will was his own composition he was a devout Christian recommending his soul "into the hands of God in whom and through the merits of Jesus Christ I trust, and believe assuredly to be saved and have full remission of my sins, and that my soul with my body, at the general day of resurrection shall rise again with joy". He named his son John and Mr. Joseph Birch executors.

The only other surviving record in which Moses Ball speaks for himself is his depositions in Alexander v. Birch, which give a favorable impression of his intelligence.

Moses Ball is said to be buried in the Ball burying ground in Clarendon. There is no marker over his grave.

---

[27] Wills Book F p. 176.

113

He has many descendants living in Virginia, West Virginia, Tennessee, Kentucky and other southern states. One of them, Mr. Palmer R. Ball has recently published a painstaking pamphlet on "The Ball Family of Southwest Virginia." Moses Ball's children, as given by him, were:

(1) John Ball born 1746 died December 1814, a soldier in the Revolution serving in the Sixth Virginia Infantry.

(2) Moses Ball, Jr. born about 1748, married Mary Ann Hardin of Fairfax County but left Fairfax before 1797 and in that year purchased a farm in Hawkins County, Tennessee.

(3) George Ball, born about 1750 died in 1839 in Russell County, Virginia. He left Fairfax County about 1795, going first to Abingdon in Washington County Virginia and then to Russell County.

(4) Bazil Ball, born about 1751 and died before 1835, in Alexandria County, leaving daughters.

(5) Ann Ball born about 1753, died unmarried.

(6) James Ball, born about 1755; date of death unknown; left a son Townsend and three daughters. It is believed that James Ball remained in Alexandria County.

(7) Sabilla Ball, born about 1757, died unmarried.

The descendants of Moses Ball now living in Arlington and Fairfax Counties trace their descent through his eldest son John Ball. He is buried in the Ball burying ground. The marker over his grave is inscribed "Ensign John Ball — Sixth Virginia Infantry Revolutionary War". Three of John Ball's sons are buried beside him; Reverend John Ball (1782–1816), Horatio Ball (1785–1872), Dabney Ball (1787–1857). A fourth son Robert Ball (1783–1861) is buried in the Central Methodist Episcopal Churchyard at Ballston. His other children were: Anna, born, it is said, December 31, 1774, married first, John Shreve, and secondly, Thomas Allison; Mary who married John Allison; William and James.

East of the Henderson woods and south of the Lee Boulevard, there stood until about twenty years ago an old brick, hip roofed dormer windowed house, known as the

"Ball" house. On the Hopkins Maps of Alexandria County (1878) it is designated as "James Ball's heirs". They were probably the heirs of James Ball, the fourth son of Moses Ball.

Late in the eighteenth century or early in the nineteenth century "Balls Tavern" was established at the crossing of the Glebe Road with the Georgetown Road and the cross roads became known as Balls Cross Roads. The tavern lot of six acres, was purchased in 1837 by Daniel Miner.

The land records do not show who occupied Moses Ball's land after his death in 1792. Presumably his widow Ann, her two daughters and perhaps his son, Bazel, continued to live there and farm it. It passed out of the family as the result of a suit filed in the chancery Court of Fairfax County. The papers are missing, but there is of record in Arlington County a deed from Colin Ault dated September 28th, 1818 to Richard Kerby[28] conveying a tract of land granted to Moses Ball containing ninety-one acres lying partly in the County of Alexandria and partly in the County of Fairfax and adjoining the patents of Simon Pearson and John Ball on the waters of Four Mile Run, which it is recited was sold under a decree of the Circuit Court of Fairfax County and purchased by said Ault. It is possible the suit was a foreclosure of the mortgage made by Moses Ball to William Wilson in 1789. At all events it terminated the seventy years connection of Moses Ball and his family, with the Glencarlyn plateau.

THE MARY CARLIN HOUSE

Shortly before his death, William Carlin made a deed of a gift of thirty-eight acres to his two infant granddaughters Mary Alexander Carlin and Ann C. Carlin, who later married Benezett. They were the children of his son

---

[28] Arlington D.B. Liber M.N. 2 – 427.

Wesley Carlin. The deed was never recorded but its existence is recited in a later deed of partition. As this parcel
has a different history from the rest of the Carlin land, I
will state here what I have ascertained about it. This was
a part of the Colville tract conveyed to Carlin by the Earl
of Tankerville and Henry A. Bennett. By a deed recorded
in 1876, [29] Mary A. Carlin and the heirs of Ann Benezett
partitioned the land. The Benezett heirs received eighteen
acres on which the Paulin, Smith and Alexander houses now
stand. Mary A. Carlin received eighteen acres. Some of
it is the property of Mrs. Kennedy but most of it is now the
property of Mr. Charles H. Lane. On that part stands an
ancient house with dormers. It is of massive hewn logs,
chinked with plaster and except for the side under the
shelter of the north porch is covered with clapboards.
Huge chimneys of brick rise at either end. Inside there is
one great chamber with fireplaces opposite each other. A
small staircase ascends to two bed rooms above. The
ceiling of the room below is crossed by heavy beams. The
house must have been built by William Carlin. Miss
Mary A. Carlin lived there until her death in 1905, having
owned it upwards of eight-five years. In her last years,
she was cared for by a faithful old colored man Joshua De
Vaughn (generally known as Uncle Josh) and his wife.
Miss Carlin gave him three acres in his lifetime, and added
three more by her will. After her death the balance of
her land was sold to Mr. Charles H. Lane who has built an
addition of colonial design which blends admirably with
the simple old dwelling.

DIVISION OF WILLIAM CARLIN'S ESTATE

William Carlin died in 1820 at the advanced age of
eighty-eight years. His will dated in 1819, is recorded in
the Clerk's Office of the City of Alexandria. [30] It begins

---

[29] Arlington D.B. Liber A-4 fol. 131.
[30] Wills Book 2 – 378,

116

with a profession of his Christian faith and directs "a descent and plain interment in my own burying ground". Though there is no tombstone over his grave he was certainly buried in the family burying lot adjoining the village library. The lot still belongs to the Carlin family. The will next directed his executors to lay off his land into small lots, likely to suit purchasers of small capital, and the proceeds, after making provision for his wife, Elizabeth, were to be divided among his heirs. He named his sons-in-law John D. Harrison and Jacob Bontz and his friend Wesley Adams executors. Wesley Adams declined to serve and the widow Elizabeth Carlin died before the settlement of the estate. The heirs were his three sons, George W. Carlin, Wesley Carlin and James Harvey Carlin, his four daughters and the children of two deceased daughters.

George W. Carlin went to Alexandria where he died in 1843. He is the ancestor of the Alexandria Carlins one of whom was a member of Congress some years ago and another a prosperous hardware merchant. Wesley Carlin and James Harvey Carlin spent their lives on parts of their father's land. The daughters named in the will were Hannah Carlin, Elizabeth Harrison, Rebecca Richards and Sarah Bontz. The other devisees were the heirs of two deceased daughters Jemima Morrison and Mary Bontz. Jacob Bontz had apparently married, first Mary Carlin, and upon her death her sister Sarah Carlin.— The executors took a long time to settle the estate and dispose of the land. Their conveyances recite two different surveys. It was found impracticable to find purchasers for the "small lots" the testator had directed his estate to be divided into. Eventually the bulk of the estate was purchased by different members of the family. The land embraced in the Gladding patent lying on both sides of Columbia Turnpike (then the "gravelled road") was the first sold and was taken over by Carlin's son-in-law, John D. Harrison. Forty-nine acres of the Lubber Run tract were taken by

John D. Richards another son-in-law.[31] In 1845 fifty-two acres of the same tract were deeded to William H. Prentiss.[32] Both of these parcels were later acquired by John B. Henderson, Jr. The remaining thirty-eight acres of the Lubber Run tract, lying east of that run and north of Four Mile Run was purchased by James Harvey Carlin,[33] and remained in the family until sold to Curtis and Burdett.

These sales left for final distribution the one hundred sixty-six acres south of Four Mile Run which constituted Carlin's purchase from the executors of John Ball. This was platted into three lots. Each of the three sons purchased a lot. Lot three containing sixty-three acres was bought by George W. Carlin of Alexandria in 1835. He conveyed it to John Bladen from whom it passed to William H. Torreyson in 1866. In 1873 Torryson sold eight acres of his tract to James Reynolds. It is located at Reynolds corner. The Benezett, the two Rice and the Howard Houses are located on it.[34]

Lot two comprising thirty-four acres lying west of the county road from Reynold's corner to Ballston was sold to Wesley Carlin about 1834. Twenty acres of this lot still belongs to the Carlin family. The other fourteen acres border Four Mile Run and is now owned by Mrs. Seaton, W. T. Ballard and Herold. In 1866 Wesley Carlin conveyed the twenty acres tract to his nephew William H. F. Carlin.[35] The large frame house on this tract is made up of two sections, built at different times. The southern and larger part was probably built by Wesley Carlin soon after 1834. The north part is an addition built by his sister, Ann E. A. Carlin about 1887.

Wesley Carlin married Catherine, whose maiden name

[31] Book 5 – 220 Arlington Land Records.
[32] Book 5 – 75 Arlington Land Records.
[33] Book 9 – 32 Arlington Land Records.
[34] Book 4 – 230 Arlington County Records.
[35] Book 9 – 139 Arlington County Records.

is not known but outlived her. Whether by accident or otherwise his first name appears in some deeds as "Westley". He was a Justice of the Peace. He died in 1875. He had two daughters, Mary Alexander Carlin who survived him, and Ann, who married Benezett and died in the lifetime of her father leaving four children, Clinton Benezett, Brittania Toner, Louisa Thom and Dallas Benezett. Mary Alexander Carlin has been already mentioned as the owner of the old Carlin house now the property of Charles H. Lane.

Lot numbered One in the division of William Carlin's house tract was bought by his son James Harvey Carlin about 1834, but the executors delayed making a deed until after his death. This lot consisted of ninety-four acres. It is identical with the subdivision of Glencarlyn, and was known as the "Mansion house tract". It has been a separate parcel and later a subdivision for the past hundred years. It appears probable that James Harvey Carlin occupied the "mansion house" from his father's death in 1820. He married Litia Skidmore sometime after 1821. He died intestate between 1844 and 1848. In the latter year Jacob Bontz and John D. Harrison, executors of of William Carlin, made a deed to Litia Carlin the widow and John E. F. Carlin, Ann E. A. Carlin, William H. F. Carlin and Andrew W. F. Carlin, in consideration of $874.00 paid by James H. Carlin deceased conveying to them "all that portion of the mansion house tract being Lot one in the division of William Carlin's estate and being a part of John Ball's patent, beginning at a white oak on the south side of Four Mile Run in the fork of a branch" – running thence west to county road; then with the county road to Four Mile Run then down the run to the beginning. The deed recites that this ninety-four acre parcel had been purchased by James H. Carlin at a public sale for $9.25 an acre, but that before a deed was executed, James H. Carlin died leaving his widow and the four children named. Of these four children, John E. F. soon moved to Washington. He lived in the southwest section of the city and kept a

119

grocery store. William H. F. Carlin in 1866 bought the land and house of his uncle Wesley and lived there until his death in 1901. Andrew (whose full name was Andrew Wilson Franklin Carlin), and Ann (whose full name was Ann Elizabeth America Carlin), lived at the old homestead. Neither of them married. Andrew Carlin turned the cleared part of the tract into a dairy and grazing farm. He had milk wagons and a milk delivery route in Washington.

RAILROADS

In 1853 the Alexandria, Loudoun and Hampshire Railway Company was chartered, and a line was surveyed running from Alexandria up the Four Mile Run Valley. The original plan was to cross the Blue Ridge and passing through Winchester to reach the coal fields of western Virginia. The money with which the road was built came mostly from Alexandria. Construction was slow and it was not until 1860 that a regular service was opened between Alexandria and Leesburg.[36] At a later date the company must have been reorganized as it bore the name of Washington, Ohio and Western Railroad Company until about 1890 when it was incorporated in the Richmond and Danville Railroad, which in turn became a part of the Southern Railway system. Connection was made with the railroad into the City of Washington by a "Y" at the intersection of the Washington, Ohio and Western with the Richmond and Danville track about two miles from Alexandria. The prosperous period of this road was from 1890 to 1905. At one time there were five passenger trains each way daily, and the cars were thronged with commuters. Among the best liked conductors were Captains King, Price and Faulkner.

---

[36] Landmarks of Old Prince William p. 593.

CARLIN SPRINGS

The railroad Company made a station on the Carlin property in the early seventies. The natural beauty of the surroundings made it a most attractive spot and the Carlins fitted it out as a picnic and excursion resort. The Hopkins atlas shows it as such before 1878. John E. F. Carlin, the son who had gone to Washington, managed the enterprise. He bricked up the two springs, built a dining and ice cream parlor capable of accommodating two hundred fifty guests, put up a dance pavilion over the bottom of the hollow between the hills and provided rustic seats and swings. A tournament course, with standards for rings was laid off in the field above the run. He also built a small bar on the narrow strip north of the railroad and south of the run. The grounds were rented for the day to excursion parties. When rented to churches and sunday schools, the bar was closed. Carlin Springs, as the resort was called, continued to be a popular resort for a dozen years, patronized by the people of Washington, Alexandria, Falls Church and the countryside, until the excursion resorts along the Potomac River drew its patrons away.

The buildings survived the sale to Curtis and Burdett and the first religious services in Glencarlyn were conducted in the old dance pavilion by students from the Virginia Theological Seminary.

Andrew W. F. Carlin died in December 1885 of pneumonia ensuing on a cold caught while delivering milk in bad weather. He devised his interest in the "old homestead estate" to his sister Ann E. A. She continued to live there for a year and half more, farming with the help of a colored helper. After the sale to Curtis and Burdett she moved to the house of her brother William on the west side of the county road and built an addition to the north end of his house, where she died in 1892. Her will directed the erection of tombstones over the graves of her brother, Andrew and her uncle Isaac P. Skidmore and his wife. The inscriptions in the graveyard are "Isaac P. Skidmore,

121

died May 1 – 1883 in the seventy-eighth year of his age". "Mary E. Skidmore, died June 1 – 1862 in the fortieth year of her age". "Andrew W. F. Carlin died December 28–1885 in the fifty-fourth year of hisage". "Sacred to the memory of Elizabeth, wife of John Dyer, died July 18th, 1869. There are other stones without inscriptions.

Other bodies known to be interred in the family plot are: the first William Carlin 1732–1820, (his will so directed and shows that the burial ground was already in existence). James Harvey Carlin, son of William; died about 1846, Litia Carlin his wife, Ann E. A. Carlin, Margetta Carlin, the wife of William H. F. Carlin. It is probable that the wives of the first William Carlin and his predeceased children are buried there. It is also probable that John Ball the original owner of the tract is buried there.

THE CARLIN HOUSE

All that remains of the old Carlin homestead is two rooms with a loft above. It is now part of a more modern house owned by Mr. Malcolm Powell. The house in which William Carlin died in 1820 was much larger and perhaps justified the description of "mansion house". The still standing structure formed its center and, I am told, had porches and closet rooms now gone. To the east was attached another smaller structure which stood until about the year 1915 when it was taken down by Mrs. Irene Young, the then owner. The central part of the house still standing is now joined on the west by a two story frame about fifty years old. This was built by Andrew W. F. Carlin. Before then its place was occupied by an old two story dormer windowed building which Andrew Carlin tore down. There were also outbuildings now gone; and there was another small house not far from the Olcott house. The dwelling house of the first William Carlin was a long frame building of eight or nine rooms, with detached outbuildings built at different times but all standing before 1800. While direct evidence is lacking, it is reasonable to suppose that the original house was begun by John Ball by the middle of the eighteenth century, and added to by William Carlin.

THE KIRBY PARCEL

I have already stated that Richard Kirby purchased Moses Ball's farm in 1818. In 1821 he granted Nehemiah Carson and Richard Veitch two-thirds of all kinds of minerals, ores or precious metals upon or within his tract, with the right to work mines and sink shafts.[37] Nothing appears to have come of the scheme. Gravel is the only mineral profitably extracted from subsoil of the tract.

Kirby never lived on the tract, it is believed, nor did any of his children. He died in 1831; by his will he devised all his property to his wife Jane for life and after her death to his seven children. What happened to the land after Richards Kirby's death is obscure. I have heard it said that James Finnecy squatted on part of it and that James Reynolds squatted on another part. This appears to be true in part. In 1851 two of Kirby's children, Sophie Elliott and Mary Kirby made an agreement to convey their interest to James Finnecy.[38] Their interest was a two-sevenths interest in remainder after the death of their mother Jane. The land was described as bounded on the east by G. W. P. Custis, on the west by the line of Fairfax County, on the north by the lands of the late James H. Carlin and on the south by the land of L. Bailey. This included all the Moses Ball patent in Alexandria County. Finnecy seems to have gone into possession, but Jane Kirby put him out by virtue of a judgment of the Circuit Court of Alexandria County entered in 1856. As she had a life estate only, this left Finnecy free to enter again on her death; and this he did.

---

[37] Book L – 2 p. 138 Arlington Land Records.
[38] Book S – 3 p. 391 Arlington Land Records.

In 1871 James Reynolds got a deed from Richard R. Kirby (son of the first Richard) which gave him a one-seventh interest.[39] Neither Finnecy or Reynolds got in the outstanding interests of the other children of Richard Kirby, but as no attack was made upon their titles, their possession in time ripened into a good and indefeasible title. In 1881 Reynolds instituted a friendly partition suit against Finnecy's heirs and so much of Moses Ball patent as lay in Alexandria County was divided between them. Reynolds was awarded the west ten and a quarter acres, comprising the Tilden Reynolds, the Isaac Reynolds and the Mima Roberts parcels.[40] The Finnecy heirs got the rest, thirty-one acres. Finnecy had died before this suit leaving a will naming children Sarah Davis, Susanna Howard, Elizabeth Stearn, Julia Davis, Virginia Runnels, Amanda Finnecy, Rosanna Finnecy and James W. Finnecy. In 1887 the Finnecy heirs divided the unsold parts of their tract into six lots and by a partitition deed[41] allotted these among themselves and their grantees. Mr. Charles Hines, Mr. Oliver H. King, Mr. Adolph Kienast, the Misses McMahon, the Misses Backus and Mrs. Backus, now own parcels, derived from the Finnecy tract. The only parts of the tract still owned by members of the family are those belonging to John Stearns and Mrs. Charles Jarboe.

FOUNDING OF GLENCARLYN

By deed of April 30th, 1887, the Carlin heirs, John E. E., Ann E. A. and William H. F., conveyed to William W. Curtis and Samuel S. Burdett[42] ninety-four acres of land "of which William Carlin died seized", excepting the family graveyard, being a part of John Ball's patent; also

---

[39] Book A – 4 p. 450 Arlington County Records.
[40] Book F – 4p. 386 Arlington County Records.
[41] Book G – 4 p. 492 Arlington County Records.
[42] Arlington D.B., D – 4 page 1.

a thirty-eight acre parcel lying east of Lubber Run and north of Four Mile Run. The purchase price was $8,000.00. This last parcel of thirty-eight acres was conveyed in 1891 by Curtis and Burdett to the Carlin Springs Company operative association, and by it to John B. Henderson, once a Senator from Missouri and, one of the seven Republican Senators who followed their consciences but committed political suicide by voting for the acquittal of President Andrew Johnson.

The reasons that induced the purchase of this particular 94 acre tract can be conjectured. It was on the line of a railroad with a fair passenger service arranged to meet the requirements of commuters. Though near Washington, it was then, and is yet, in a real sense, in the country, surrounded by woods, streams and farms.

Its setting was a level plateau formed by the confluence of two brooks. The railroad approach from Arlington Station (now Barcroft) followed the deep gorge of Four Mile Run where the water rippled and tumbled by turns over a rocky bottom. There is hardly a more beautiful mile in Northern Virginia. The smaller brook, Long Branch, is a miniature of the larger one, making its way through a deep and rocky valley. The hill slopes overlooking the two streams were not suitable home building sites, but could be advantageously converted into a park for the proposed subdivision. Arlington County is an old community, as we count age in the United States. Its settlement goes back to 1700. Glencarlyn is a late episode in its history, but it was, I believe, the first subdivision in the county deliberately planned in advance. Even Alexandria grew out of a settlement around the Hunting Creek tobacco warehouse. Rosslyn, Hall's Hill and East Falls Church were small communities, before Glencarlyn existed, but they grew up in a haphazard fashion. Our county is now a congery of subdivisions. There is hardly a farm left, but as late as 1887, the county, outside of Alexandria was predominately rural and agricultural.

The founders of our community, having a clean slate,

could lay off a compact rectangular village, with straight streets and lots of uniform size, and plan its development in advance. Their problem was to secure the right sort of purchasers. It was not then the fashion to bind the lots of a subdivision by uniform restrictive covenants, but Curtis and Burdett had definite ideas as to desirable residents for their village. The first prospectus issued was addressed "To all men and women of moderate means or who receive stated salaries". The home builders desired were mainly government clerks; persons of some education, refinement and congenial tastes, capable of building up a small homogeneous community. When the lots were offered for sale, most of the early purchasers bought several contiguous lots. Many who expected to build were unable to do so, or changed their minds. It is to this happy combination of design and accident that Glencarlyn owes its most pleasant and distinctive characteristic. Its houses lie widely spread out over its sixty acres of platted land.

To return to the prospectus: This little pamphlet set out seductively the attractions of the new village; its nearness to Washington, the convenient railroad facilities, landing the future resident in the heart of the city in twenty-five minutes; the healthful character of the neighborhood; the groves of primitive oaks, and the picturesque dells, the charming watercourses that ran through the proposed park. But the attraction most stressed was the co-operative plan of the proposed village — each buyer of a lot was to receive a share in a syndicate to be composed of all the lot owners. All land not subdivided was to be turned over to this syndicate, as well as the Carlin homestead. It took more than a year to grade and subdivide the tract; to lay off streets and lots, and to mark their boundaries, to plant young trees, mostly maples, and generally to prepare a saleable subdivision. Twenty-four blocks were laid off, divided into three hundred eighty-four lots, of which three hundred sixty were offered for sale. The name originally given the subdivision was "Carlin Springs", and the lots have been uniformly conveyed, and are still conveyed, as lots of Curtis and Burdett's subdivision of Carlin Springs. Some thirty acres of the tract lying south of Four Mile Run were not included in the platted subdivision. The lots were sold at $100.00 apiece, cash or monthly instalments. This continued to be the standard price until the nineteen-twenties. The first deed to a purchaser (Robert L. Ewing) was recorded on October 3rd, 1888, and a plat of the subdivision was attached to and recorded with it.[43] In the course of the next three months deeds were recorded conveying upwards of fifty lots. Among the first purchasers were William M. King, Solon W. Stocking, William M. Backus, Laura E. Jones, James M. Loughlin, Henry B. Hedrick and Charles A. Mason.

CARLIN SPINGS CO-OPERATIVE ASSOCIATION

Before putting the lots on the market, a subsidiary corporation was chartered in 1888 under the name of the Carlin Springs Co-operative Association to carry into effect the representations made in the prospectus. The capital stock was $16,000.00 divided into three hundred sixty shares with a par of $50.00 each. Its purposes were declared to be to acquire land at or near Carlin Springs; to improve it by laying it out into parks, gardens and building lots; to erect houses, outhouses and hotels. Other objects enumerated — possibilities rather than probabilities, — were to build telegraph and telephone lines between Carlin Springs and Washington, and elsewhere, and to establish stage or coach lines between the same points, and to operate them for the profit and benefit of the stockholders.

The assets of the corporation consisted of the Carlin homestead; seventy-four acres of unsubdivided land; $2,000.00 paid in by Curtis and Burdett. The subsequent sale in 1894 to ex-senator Henderson of thirty-eight of these seventy-four acres for $3,750.00 gave the association

[43] Arlington D.B., J-4 folio 63.

127

additional funds. The minutes of the association show many expenditures for the improvement of the park and streets of the village; also loans to assist in building houses. The association never built a house on its own account.

In 1890 it had prepared a plat showing the existing subdivision and a proposed addition, to be known as First Addition to Carlin Springs, by which it was proposed to dedicate thirteen acres for a park, and lay off the remaining twenty acres belonging to it into blocks lettered "A" to "L", subdivided into lots. The park land lay along the south bank of Four Mile Run, and the lettered blocks on the long slopes above the run. Names were assigned to different parts of the park, "West End", "Round Top", "The Glen", "Springmont", "The Holm", and "The Cape". These fanciful names never took. This plat was printed, and is the standard reference map of the village and the park. It was not until 1897, however, that the First Addition and dedication was recorded.[44] The lettered blocks were then changed so as to be "A" to "I'", and the park divisions were named "West End", "The Glen", "Central Park", "Springmont", and "East End Park".

In 1898 the park land was deeded by the Association to William M. Backus to hold for the use and benefit of the lot owners until the Legislature of the State of Virginia should grant a charter of incorporation to the town of Glencarlyn incorporating it into a municipality, town or body politic, "which is contemplated in the near future" — an anticipation that has never been realized —, when the trustee was directed to convey to such municipal corporation.

Very few of the lots in the lettered blocks were sold. In 1923 the Association conveyed the balance of them and the original park land to Mr. James H. Schaaff to hold in trust for the use and benefit of the people of Glencarlyn as a park,[44] thus bringing the total park area up to about thirty acres. Mr. Schaaff died in 1933. No trustee has

---

[44] Arlington D.B., U – 4 p. 224.
[45] Arlington D.B., 196 – 275.

been substituted in his place. In the same year — 1923 — the Association wound up its existence by voluntary dissolution. Its assets were upward of $9,400.00 cash. This divided rateably among its stockholders of over $25.00 a share. These were the original lot owners, their heirs, or assigns. It was not possible to locate all of them, and about $1,000.00 was deposited in the Clerk's office of the County, to await proof of ownership, where it still is, or should be, for an untoward fate has overtaken much money deposited in the Office of the County Clerk.

The plat of the First addition is interesting because it shows also the original subdivision with the houses built there by the year 1890; less than two years after the sale of the first lot. It shows fourteen new dwelling houses in addition to the Carlin house. Five of them were on the south side of Laurel Street. They were: (1) the house now owned by Carl Schulze, (2) the one now occupied by Mr. Mazi and owned by Mrs. McMahon, (5) the house built by Captain Pennywit and now owned by Mrs. Harrison, (4) the house built by the late H. W. Olcott, burned, rebuilt, and still owned by the Olcott family, (5) the house built by Henry Hedrick, later burned and its site now occupied by the house of Judge Benjamin Hedrick. Five houses were shown on Maple Street. They were: (6) the house now owned by the Loughlin family, (7) the Burdett house now owned by Mrs. Frank Hester, (8) the Carlin house now owned by Mr. Powell, (10) the house now occupied by Mr. Bechtl and built by B. T. Janney, (11) one house was shown on Poplar Street, that built by the late M. C. Mitchell and now owned by his daughter Mrs. Brewer. Four houses appear on Walnut Street (12) the house built by Laura E. Jones and now owned by Oliver H. King, (13) the house built by Mr. Stockbridge afterward burned, and the site now occupied by the house of Mr. Adolph Kienast, (14) a house burned many years ago located near the house owned by the Misses McMahon, (15) the house built by Dr. Wm. M. Backus and now owned by his daughters. From this recital it appears that the "ancient

129

planters" of Glencarlyn are the Olcott, Hedrick, Loughlin, Brewer and Backus families.

The name of the village was changed to Glencarlyn early in 1896 at the instance of the co-operative association. Its minutes show that in 1888, before the subdivision was made, three names were proposed — "Glenn Carlin" by Mr. Janney; "Carlin Heights" by Major King, and "Carlin Springs" by Mr. Howard; the last chosen by a majority vote.

The building now used as a school house was built in 1892 by the Carlin Hall Association, a stock corporation composed of lot owners. It was named "Curtis Hall" in honor of William W. Curtis, one of the founders of the village, and served by turns as a place of social gathering, a church, and a school. It was purchased from the hall association by the co-operative association in May 1896. About ten years ago it was turned over to the County upon condition that it be used for school purposes only.

THE BURDETT LIBRARY

This handsome building is the gift of General S. S. Burdett to the people of the village. His will bequeathed to Dr. William M. Backus a large lot styled The Reservation, an adjoining lot, and a portion of his residuary estate, (which ultimately amounted to $14,000.00); his interest in the unsold Curtis and Burdett lots, and his library, in trust to erect on the Reservation a library building, to be used as a public library for the use of the inhabitants of Glencarlyn and its vicinity, to maintain such building and to purchase books, pamphlets and magazines for the betterment and extension of the library. The custody of a part of this fund was entrusted in a trust company in Washington, from which the library receives the interest. Dr. Backus died before building the library and was succeeded in the trusteeship by his son Curtis B. Backus who built the library at a cost of about $7,000.00. The present trustees are Constance A. Backus, Margaret T. Olcott and Charles W. Stetson. The Library owns a one-half interest in twenty-two lots in the village and its endowment fund is about $9,000.00, of which $1,000.00 is the gift of Mrs. Elizabeth B. Gifford, in memory of her husband, Reverend Nelson Davis Gifford, a beloved student of the Virginia Theological Seminary who served St. John's Chapel from 1923 to 1926 — The Library contains about 4,000 books.

ST. JOHN'S CHAPEL

For many years there was no church building in the village, but the Virginia Theological Seminary near Alexandria, established a mission as soon as enough houses had been built to justify it. When the town hall was built in 1892 services were conducted there by students assigned to the mission by the seminary. A long succession of earnest, gifted young men — many now rectors of large congregations, and some bishops — have conducted their first services, and preached their first sermons in Glencarlyn. About 1910 St. John's Chapel was built, with money raised in large part by the devoted efforts of Mrs. Laura E. Jones, now deceased. In 1921 a tower was added. The exterior of the chapel is not notable, and does not prepare the visitor for its beautiful and truly religious interior. The congregation has never been numerous or prosperous enough to afford a rector of its own; it is still served by students from the seminary.

THE FOUNDERS OF GLENCARLYN

This sketch may fittingly conclude with a brief notice of the founders of Glencarlyn, William Wallace Curtis and Samuel Swinfin Burdett. Both were notable men.

The former was born in Ohio in 1828 of Revolutionary descent. He married Jane L. Backus, came to Washington in 1861 and made his home in Georgetown. During the Civil War he was a special correspondent for the New York Times and through his field glasses watched the encounter between the Monitor and the Merrimac, of which he wrote an account printed in the Times. He was one of the guard of honor at President Lincoln's bier in the rotunda of the Capitol. He was a man of cultivated tastes, something of an artist, a poet and a musician; and was at one time President of the board of trustees of the public schools of Washington. The Curtis School in Georgetown perpetuates his name. He formed a partnership with General S. S. Burdett for the practice of land law. He died just as the Carlin Springs subdivision was launched. The management of his interest devolved on his talented son Mr. Charles William Curtis now of Rochester, New York.

General Burdett (as he was universally called) lived for a quarter of a century in the village he founded. He was born in England in 1836, the son of a Baptist Minister and was himself intended for the ministry. When twelve years old he was sent to the United States in company with an older brother. It was his father's expectation to follow with the rest of his family, but his death prevented; and the young English emigrant was left to his own resources. He began the struggle of life in Ohio, working on a farm in summer and attending school in winter. Somehow he worked his way through Oberlin College, and at the outbreak of the Civil War was in Iowa, beginning the practice of law. He enlisted in the Union army; served three years and came out as captain of Company B, First Iowa Cavalry. He then went to Missouri, married and rose rapidly in his profession. He was a member of Congress from that state from 1869 to 1873 and Commissioner of the General Land Office in Washington from 1874 to 1876. He was active in the affairs of the Grand Army of the Republic and at one time its Commander in Chief. Ever after he was called "General" by friends and acquaintances. On account of ill health, he started on a tour around the world in June 1876, in which he visited England, the southwestern coast

of Africa, the island of St. Helena, Australia, returning by
way of the Hawaiian Islands to San Francisco where he
arrived in August 1877, perfectly restored to health. Soon
after he became a member of the law firm of Curtis, Earle
and Burdett.–The rest of his long life he spent in Washington and Glencarlyn. His house was one of the first built
in the village. It is now the home of Mrs. Frank Hester.
For some years he maintained a winter residence in Washington, but in his later life spent the whole year in our
village, except when travelling. He was the first President
of the Carlin Springs Co-operative Association and gave
freely of his time and energy to the promotion of the
interests and welfare of the village. The minute book of
the Association contains his annual reports to the stockholders written in longhand and pasted in the book. They
show his bright hopes for the speedy growth of the village
and the increase in land values, with caustic comments on
"the unjustifiable and even unnatural expansion" of rival
subdivisions then springing up "most of which never got
beyond the paper stage and are now confessed failures".

But General Burdett's greatest gift to Glencarlyn was
the simple, unaffected life he lived among us. He was
interested in the lives of his neighbors, and his sympathy,
counsel, and at need, his financial assistance, were freely
given. Political ambition had passed away, and he learned
a genuine affection for his adopted state and its historic
past.

Always a reader, his books were the solace of his old
age. He had the interesting habit of making marginal
comments on books he read. On one of his books, now in
the village library, treating controversial religious subjects
from an orthodox point of view, the first ten or fifteen pages
abound in emphatic pencilled dissents. "The rest is
silence". Evidently, the General stopped there, too dis-
gusted to read more. The fiction in his library was negli-
gible. Solid sets of Darwin, Tyndall, Huxley and Spencer
show the influences that moulded his intellectual life.
Though not a church goer, he gave liberally to the chapel in

133

the village, and was always deeply interested in religious questions. I remember how fascinated he was by the modernist movement in the Roman Catholic Church, eagerly following its development in the works of Loisy, Tyrrell and others. He died before he realized its inevitable failure. He told the writer of being once called on to address an assembly of Baptists in San Francisco. In the course of his remarks, he developed the general theme of tolerance. If, he said, you should travel in the mountains of Tibet and came across one of those humble prayer mills that are found in Buddhist lands, don't pass it by with contempt. "Stop; give it a push."

A SHIPWRECK

General Burdett traveled much. In August 1909 he embarked at Seattle in the steamship Ohio for Alaska. The boat took the inner passage between the islands and the mainland. At midnight it struck a rock, tearing a great hole in its bottom. The captain with coolness and skill ran for a little cove or bay and succeeded in grounding the ship on a ledge of rock while the passengers put on life belts and the crew launched the life boats. The General later recounted his experience at a reception tendered him on his return by the Legion of Loyal Women. The proceedings were printed in a pamphlet now in our library from which I quote an extract:

"Fortunately the water was calm. The embarcation began, first the women and children: then the men. Was there eager rushing? Yes, eagerness, but not actual rushing. There were strong men there to do the part of manly men, not forgetful of duty. There was but one attempt to have a place among the embarking women. I do not care to dwell on that. One by one the boats were filled and vanished into the darkness. It was not hard to embark, the ship was low in the water. The last boat on which I saw any take refuge was full, very full, so it seemed

134

to my old eyes in that darkness. It might have been better judgment on my part to have stepped over her side, to have crowded in with the rest, but I did not. The water was then over my feet. I shall challenge your credulity by saying that there were moments of calm pleasure at that crisis of fate. When the boat vanished there was no other human being within my sight. So far as I then knew, and rejoiced to know all the others were on the road to safety. As afterward learned there were five, who imprisoned between decks had already met death ....As that last boat vanished from sight, the great ship careened, bringing the water above my waist and then settled down deeply to her stern........I was drawn down and, as I think at first to her stern; then there came along a rush of water which carried me forward and out, clear of the wreck......a return wave carried me back to and over the wreck and left me beneath the surface, where for a moment or two I was held by an entanglement about my feet, perhaps the floating tackle by which the boats had been suspended from their davits. Rest seemed very near just then. The air was expelled from my lungs. The water entered. There were no stars to bid me good night. The blackness of darkness was above and the waters for a winding sheet. But the little ones were by their mother's side on the nearby shore ....The Eternal was in his place. . Perhaps the physical struggle which impending suffocation caused freed me from the cruel entanglement. I found myself half conscious at the surface, and floated there until a returning boat, look-ing for human wreckage, picked me up."

A newspaper item in the Philadelphia Ledger of September 12, 1909, states the real reason why he "stood aside and refused to enter the boats, because as he said, other men had thirty or forty years to expect, and their lives were valuable, whereas, at his age, seventy-four, a man could expect at the most only a few more years of existence."

Shortly after the World War began he returned to visit the scenes of his boyhood life in England and on

135

September 14, 1914 he died while visiting his old home, The Manse, Broughton, Astler, Leicestershire.

It is believed by his friends that he felt his end was approaching and returned to die at his birthplace.

The words that Shakespeare puts into the mouth of Cassius, are appropriate to the death of General Burdett:

"Time is come around, and where I did begin, there shall I end. My life is run his compass".

His remains were brought back to this country, and he lies buried beside his wife in Arlington Cemetery.

INDEX

137

140

141

www.ingramcontent.com/pod-product-compliance
Lightning Source LLC
Chambersburg PA
CBHW070449090426
42735CB00012B/2494